NATIONALISM IN SOUTH ASIA

NATIONALISM IN SOUTH ASIA

RAJESH RAI
SUNIL KUKREJA

Ashwin-Anoka Press
New Delhi/Kuala Lumpur

First Published – 2009

ISBN: 978-81-904750-3-7

Published by

ASHWIN-ANOKA PRESS
New Delhi-110002, (India)

Branch Office

4830/24, Prahlad Street,
Ansari Road, Darya Ganj,
New Delhi-110002, (India)
Phone : 23245225 Fax : 91-11-23272135
E-mail: serials@satyam.net.in

CONTENTS

CONTRIBUTORS LIST

Rajesh Rai, Assistant Professor at the South Asian Studies Programme, National University of Singapore, completed his Ph.D. at the School of Historical Studies at the University of Birmingham.His research interests are in the fields of nationalism and the postcolonial history and politics of South Asia, diaspora studies and transnational identities. Among the books he has edited are (with Peter Reeves) of The South Asian Diaspora: Transnational Networks and Changing Identities (London: Routledge, 2008); and (with Brij V. Lal and Peter Reeves) The Encyclopedia of the Indian Diaspora (Singapore: Editions Didier Millet, 2006).

Dagmar Hellmann-Rajanayagam, studied History, Tamil Philology and Comparative Religion at the universities of Hamburg and Heidelberg (South Asia Institute). M.A. 1978, Ph.D. 1982, D. Litt. 1998. She has taught and researched in Heidelberg, Kiel, Oxford, London, Chennai, Colombo, Singapore, Kuala Lumpur, Erlangen, Kiel, and is currently Reader at University of Passau, Department of Southeast Asian Studies.

Shapan Adnan, was educated at the Universities of Sussex and Cambridge, and undertook research at Queen Elizabeth House (University of Oxford). He currently teaches in the South Asian Studies Programme at the National University of Singapore, and has previously taught at the Universities of Dhaka and Chittagong in Bangladesh.

Ishtiaq Ahmed, is a Professor of Political Science (Stockholm University) and Visiting Senior Research Fellow at the Institute of South Asian Studies, National University of Singapore.

Rajshree Jetly, is a Research Fellow at the Institute of South Asian Studies, an institute at the National University of Singapore (NUS). She has a Ph.D. in Political Science and International

Relations (Australian National University, Canberra), a Masters in South Asian Studies (Jawaharlal Nehru University), and a Masters and Bachelors in History (Delhi University).

Mahmoud 'Max' Kashefi, is professor of Sociology at Eastern Illinois University. He received his Ph.D. from Indiana University, and his areas of expertise include Social Statistics, Social Change, Sociology of Work and Occupations, and Social Organization.

1

INTRODUCTION: SOUTH ASIAN NATIONALISMS

RAJESH RAI

Fifty-one countries signed the Charter of the United Nations (UN) when it was established on 26 June 1945. Since then, the world has witnessed two successive waves of nationalism. The first, commencing in the aftermath of the Second World War and extending to the early 1980s, was tied to the dissolution of colonial empires in the developing world. The war had crippled European powers militarily and economically, and the very ideology that justified colonialism had come to be severely undermined. Challenged by the advance of national liberation movements, and lacking the political will to offer sustained resistance, the end of colonial rule saw in its wake the emergence of a multitude of newly independent states in Asia, Africa and the Caribbean. In the late-1980s, a second wave of nationalism grew out of the political and economic changes that took place in the Soviet-bloc. *Perestroika* and *Glasnost*, which [unintentionally] led to the overthrow of communist regimes in Eastern Europe and the Soviet Union, also provided "A new lease of life... into hitherto dormant volcanoes of nationalism" (Sathyamurthy, 1998: 2250). The unification of Germany in October 1990 and the dramatic collapse of the Soviet Union in December 1991, which splintered into 15 independent states (Phadnis & Ganguly, 2001:16), remain the most poignant memories of those turbulent years. They ushered a wider surge of ethnic nationalism in the region, whose embers have since continued to dwell in the array of ethno-national movements in the Balkans, and the Caucasus. In 2006, largely as a result of these two waves of nationalism since the Second World War, the count of UN's list of member states had expanded nearly four-fold, to 192 (United Nations, 2006).

The exponential increase of member states of the UN may be astonishing, but it does not provide an adequate testimony of nationalism's pervasiveness. Only a small proportion of all nationalist movements in fact 'succeed' in making the UN's privileged list. A far greater number have either been placated or suppressed, or continue to be resisted in the erstwhile states where they have arisen. Moreover, while nationalist movements that seek liberation and secession have tended to draw greater public attention, these should not be mistaken as the only form that nationalism takes. More quiescent processes that generate loyalty and erode sub-national affinities for the purpose of maintaining order and promoting development in the process of 'nation-building' are certainly more ubiquitous, and play a crucial role in the socialization processes of citizens (Breuilly, 1985: 234). Other non-secessionist varieties of nationalism have been more vociferous, possibly due to the desire for a change in the national 'settlement' to reflect more closely the demands of the majority, or because of concerns over immigration, which has, in recent years sparked right-wing nationalist responses even in the more mature nations in Western Europe (Phadnis & Ganguly, 2001: 16). Such developments in turn have provoked minorities "to politically mobilise themselves in order to protect and promote their political, economic and socio-cultural rights" (16), and where a minority group is geographically concentrated and has strong historical ties in a specific region these may very well trigger reactionary calls for a separate and independent homeland.

Making Sense of Nationalism

The resilience, pervasiveness and virility of nationalism in the twentieth century has been matched by studies of nationalism "so vast and interdisciplinary as to rival all other contemporary foci of intellectual production" (Verdery, 1993: 37). Incorporating anthropology, sociology, psychology along with the traditional domains of history and political science, these works have sought to shed new light to the old overarching questions of what nationalism is, the reasons for its emergence and why it remains so pervasive. While these scholarly works have provided analytical depth to the understanding of nationalism, attempts at theorizing this phenomenon have been a subject of considerable debate. Tamir notes that:

> Critics of recent philosophical analyses of nationalism suggest that nationalism is a unique social phenomenon that cannot, and need not be theorized. Are there, indeed, some special features constitutive of nationalism that might defy theorization? Those answering this question in the affirmative point to the plurality and specificity of national experiences, as well as to the emotional and eclectic nature of nationalist discourse (1999: 67).

Such aspersions to theorization are certainly legitimate to the extent that issues of identity and culture, which form critical components of nationalism, "...are not the ideal variables of social 'science'" given their "amorphous and intangible nature..." (Romano, 2006: 17). The attempt to understand the complexity of nationalism, however, can be made more manageable if one breaks down the phenomenon into its constituent elements. Anthony Smith defines nationalism as "an ideological movement for the attainment and maintenance of autonomy, unity and identity on behalf of a population some of whose members deem themselves to constitute an actual or potential 'nation'" (1996: 447). While Smith's definition underscores nationalism as an ideology and as a movement, the starting point for a critical understanding requires an appreciation of the operative term 'nation' and an awareness of the debates that surround the concept.

Scholars of nationalism agree that "Nation is a form of identity" and that "Individuals identify with their nation in the same way that they might identify with other forms of collective identity" (Dawisha, 2002: 3). Beyond this however, there is dispute "over the constituent elements of a nation and interplay between and among these elements" (3). Alongside a common will and consent, questions are posed as to whether, and the extent to which, markers of identity such as, ethnicity, 'race', religion, language and historical memory are crucial markers of a nation.

The antecedents of this debate go back to at least the mid-nineteenth century when "ideas [of nation] were clustered into two main intellectual strands" (6). Influenced by Romanticism, the German conception, viewed the nation as "organic beings, living personalities, whose individuality must be cherished by [its] members in all their manifestations. The nation [is founded] not on 'mere' consent or law but on passions implanted by nature and history" (Hutchinson (1989) cited in Dawisha, 2002: 7). The Anglo-Saxon model, on the other hand rejected the idea of the nation's 'immemorial past' instead emphasizing the role of the state, its government and laws in the development of a collective national consciousness (10-13). It's more liberal advocates underscored free will and consent in affiliation, pointing out that "the nation cannot be forced on any individual or group;... [and] there is nothing that is predetermined or preordained about the concept" (14). In the contemporary period, the two strands continue to be reflected in "The ethnic idea of the nation [that]... celebrates inherited cultural identity and is exemplified by Germany, Japan, and most Eastern European countries" and "The civic idea of the nation [that] in contrast, is... the freely chosen and purely political identity of participants in such modern states as France, Canada, and the United States" (Yack, 1999: 103).

For scholars of nationalism, the 'ethnic' and 'civic' models of nation provide a yardstick upon which to assess the nation's constituent identities, and the degree to which national ideologies are exclusive or inclusive. In accounting for the emergence and development of nations and nationalism, scholars have adopted a number of approaches that have been influenced by the two dominant strands of political thought on the 'nation' set out above. These can be categorized into the primordial and ethno-symbolist approaches on the one hand, and modernization theories and the instrumentalist approach on the other.

The primordial school's approach draws from the Germanic conception, and emphasizes the pre-modern attributes of 'nation'. Predictably, nationalists have been the most active proponents of primordialism and their discourse has also often been the crudest representation of this approach. In nationalist discourse, not only has the nation or the dominant ethnic community that forms the core of the nation existed since time immemorial, but as well that their identity has remained largely unchanged through the ages. Nationalism thus occurs as a natural expression of the nation's desire for freedom and control over the territory which they claim to be their historic homeland. Needless to say, such representations have been found to be at variance with historical evidence (Breuilly, 1996: 150-1), and lack explanatory value in terms of how these 'nations' were formed in the first place. Even Smith, a scholar sympathetic to some primordialist claims points out that

> Primordialism per se is untenable, since it assumes what is to be explained: why human beings are so widely differentiated by ethnic origin and culture. It fails to explain why particular ethnic communities emerge, change and dissolve, or why so many people choose to emigrate and assimilate to other ethnies (Smith, 1996: 446).

While the primordial approach has been subject to severe criticism, the recent upsurge in ethno-nationalist movements, have posed questions as to whether the contentions of primordialism can be summarily dismissed. In his influential work *The Ethnic Origins of Nations* (1986) Smith's 'ethno symbolist' approach provides a more sophisticated explanation that draws from the primordial school. Smith argues that the primary reason for the resilience of certain ethnies is the presence of 'myth-symbol' complexes, for example a religion with its own customs, sacred language, holy texts and organized priesthood (Tonneson & Antlov, 1996: 9). He underscores that the study of nationalism, therefore must begin with the study of the core ethnic community because these provided the foundations upon which states were formed before gradually becoming nation states:

> The other ethnie were drawn into the dominant ethnic culture of the state, and accepted to some extent its history as their own... those that were not so acculturated, were left in a neglected and subordinate position (Smith 1986: 139-40).

Scholars who emphasize the primordial/ethno-symbolist approach to nationalism provide important insights as to why affective attachments prove such powerful motivations in nationalist movements. These studies also help explain why "nations are endowed with a very special psychological dimension–an emotional dimension–not enjoyed by essentially functional or juridical grouping... such as socio-economic classes or states" (Connor 1994: 74). Even modernization theorists increasingly acknowledge that primordial ethnic identity can have some role in the creation and nature of nationalist movements. Nonetheless, they question the viability of studying primordial ties as they contend that it is difficult to co-relate "the objective importance of... myths and symbols" and the degree of success of politicians who "weave these into arguments designed to promote national identity" (Breuilly, 1996: 150). They also point out that the primordial approach does not deal sufficiently with the problem of shifting and mutating tendencies of ethnic groupings in its attempt at broad-based mobilization and assimilation, its association and competition with other ethnic groupings as well as in its struggle towards nationhood resulting in multiple pressures to redefine itself (Pieterse, 1997: 365-9).

While primordialism can help explain the emotional strength in nationalist movements, "the sufficient conditions for strong and widespread nationalism are more difficult to identify" (Kellas, 1991: 34). A vast array of modernisation theories identify these conditions as an outcome of political and socio-economic changes that have occurred in modernity, which act as key catalysts in fostering nationalism and the construction of nations. According to these theories "nationalism is an explicitly modern ideology and movement, that is to say, it is both novel and relatively recent" (Smith, 2000: 4).

Gellner's influential work, *Nations and Nationalism* (1983), posits that nationalism emerges out of the socio-economic changes that take place in the process of industrialization. Nationalism, he argues "is a reflection of the basic social organization of industrial and industrializing people" (Gellner, 1994: 29) since industrial society, which witnesses far greater mobility than agrarian societies, depends upon a common culture, a homogeneous education system and a vernacular language for its communication needs. According to Gellner, nationalism is generated when there exist differences in terms of access to power and education for certain groups in the process of homogenizing pre-modern identities to produce a standard national culture. Marxist interpretations of nationalism come close to Gellner's position, although their focus has been on nationalism's drive against imperialism. Their argument essentially posits that because capitalism's expansion globally has been asymmetrical, nationalism has emerged as a "natural response of the disadvantaged regions, much as socialism is for the oppressed classes" (Munck, 1986: p. 146).

Anderson's *Imagined Communities* (1991) views the 'nation' as "an imagined political community... imagined as both inherently limited and sovereign" (Anderson, 1991: 6). Anderson's point is not that all communities (with the exception of traditional villages where people meet face to face) are 'imagined', rather he posits that the crucial question is why this distinct style of imagining came about. He underscores that the nation is imagined "as *limited* because even the largest of them... has finite, if elastic, boundaries, beyond which lie other nations"; "as *sovereign* because the concept was born in an age in which Enlightenment and Revolution were destroying the legitimacy of the divinely ordained, hierarchical dynastic realm"; "as a *community*, because, regardless of the actual inequality and exploitation that may prevail in each, the nation is always conceived as a deep, horizontal comradeship" (7). Crucial in Anderson's account is the importance of the changes that occurred in print capitalism, particularly in the form of newspapers published in the vernacular that "created the possibility of a new form of imagined community, which in it's basic morphology set the stage for the modern nation" (36). As a result, Anderson argues, three modular forms of nationalism–creole, vernacular and official–shaped in America and Europe emerged, and came to be transplanted to the colonies in the middle and late nineteenth century.

Breuilly's approach in *Nationalism and the State* (1985), argues that it is political action that transforms ethnic communities into nations. According to Breuilly, nationalism emerged largely as an outcome of the revolutionary changes that took place in France in the late eighteenth century which

> conditioned the development of politics as a special activity of general interest. Elections, party organization, a politics aiming to shape 'public opinion'... As the state became the object of mass public attention, it appealed to this public in national terms. Those who rejected the national legitimacy claimed by the existing state themselves resorted to nationalist arguments.... Increased state intervention in such fields as education and social welfare bound ever larger groups to the state and promoted a common, 'national' culture' (Breuilly, 2001: 38).

While Breuilly's approach concentrates on the emergence of the modern state in explaining the advent of nationalism, through it's emphasis on the role of the political elite it also sets the base for the instrumentalist reading of nationalism. Brass, an exponent of the instrumentalist approach posits that "the study of ethnicity and nationality is in large part the study of politically-induced cultural change" (Brass, 1991: 75). In this reading, the psychological and emotional aspects of collective identities have tended not to be emphasized rather the instrumentalist approach has focused on the political elite's 'manipulation' of identities, alongside their resource mobilization strategies including "material interest-based appeals, as well as strategic use of recruitment network... [that] serve as the crucial extra inducement to action" (Romano, 2006: 67). While initially these works focused on the 'producers' of nationalism, more sophisticated theories have since emerged that highlight the need to look as well at the potential participants in a nationalist movement. Drawn from economic theories, the rational choice arguments *vis-à-vis* nationalism essentially posit that "unless individuals are given rational, self-interested reasons for supporting or joining a movement..., the movement will fail to attract a mass following, reducing the movement's choices to either very small scale actions... or failure" (68).

Collectively, modernization and instrumentalist theories have been extremely influential in the study of nationalism, and offer a wide-range of analytical tools for research. Useful in accounting for temporal and focal changes in nationalist movements, they have come to provide important insight to issues such as, for example, the impact of the development of communications or of urbanization on nationalism or whether power-sharing in multi-cultural states tends to encourage or discourage ethno-national movements. Scholars who underscore the importance of ethnicity and the need for a longer reading of the formation of nations and nationalism, nevertheless point out that the modernization and instrumentalist approaches on their own are insufficient. Instrumentalism's weakness, according to Smith, is that it cannot provide an explanation for the intensity of ethnic conflicts and "why so many people may be ready to lay down their lives for their nations" (Smith, 1996: 446). Similarly he argues that modernization accounts are inadequate because they provide "only one half... of the story. The other half, the fact that so many modern nations have been built on the foundation of pre-existing ethnies and so many ethnic nationalisms can draw on ethnic sentiments and shared memories, myths, symbols and values, is omitted..." (446).

Nationalism in South Asia

Few defining moments in history have better personified the antipathetic guise of nationalism than the independence of two of the largest states in South Asia[1]–India and Pakistan–in August 1947. India's nationalist struggle against colonial exploitation and servitude–laconically portrayed in the image of that half-naked man with a walking stick, leading a *Satyagraha* against the forces of the British empire–would resonate long after, in distant civic and anti-colonial struggles for freedom and equality. Yet, at the juncture intended to mark the realization of that journey, celebrations were muted. Freedom came at a price. Partition, the solution of an Empire seeking an early exit in the face of competing nationalisms, left in it's wake a bestial carnage of religious violence hitherto unseen in South Asia, with some two million Hindu, Muslims and Sikh dead, and an "estimated 12-15 million... forcibly transferred between the two countries" (Ahmed, 2002: 9).

Over the last 60 years, South Asia has seen a discernible, albeit gradual and haphazard, move in the direction of greater democracy. Democratic change in most South Asian states, has come to be reflected not only in the evolution of a more stable electoral process, but also in the establishment of both state-led and non-governmental civic institutions aimed at protecting the rights of its people. Monarchies, the dominant model of state authority throughout the long history of South Asia, have all but been abolished even in the more insulated states in the region. In Nepal, this has taken the form of a Maoist-led movement that eventually brought to an end the Rana dynasty in late 2007. The last remaining bastion of monarchy in South Asia, the tiny mountainous kingdom of Bhutan, saw parliamentary elections being held for the first time in early 2008. In the Maldives, where the monarchy was removed as far back as 1968, the institutionalization of participant democracy has been a long-drawn process and the first multi-party elections were held only in late 2008.

Notwithstanding these political changes, the recent history of South Asia has also witnessed developments that have severely questioned the viability of the modern nation-state. In a region that accounts for nearly one-quarter of the world's population, South Asia is a mosaic of ethnic and religious communities. It comes as no surprise that these plural states have remained vulnerable to challenges from ethnic and religious nationalist movements. Possibly nowhere in South Asia has the power of ethnic nationalism been more deeply personified than in Sri Lanka. Over the last three decades, a state once deemed by the British as a 'model' colony, has been torn apart by a civil war formed out of the opposing forces of Tamil and Sinhala nationalism. Meanwhile, in the Islamic Republics of Iran and Afghanistan, fundamentalist forms of religious nationalism have remained the most virile sources of identification, and in the latter, the Taliban continues–in spite of the US-led offensive after September 11–to be a major threat to the development of democratic institutions in the state.

In India's case, ethnic and religious diversity is so great that the journalist and scholar Selig Harrison in 1960 predicted the possibility of its territorial demise: "The odds are almost wholly against the survival of freedom and... the issue is, in fact, whether any Indian state can survive at all" (Harrison, 1960: 338). Although compared to many of its neighbours, nation-building in India based on a secular civic-territorial model, has been relatively successful, this has not been without significant challenges. Even as India was able to stave off threats from the 'Dravidistan' movement in the South by reorganizing it's federal system along linguistic states in 1956 (Kohli, 1997: 334), by the 1980s it faced even more serious secessionist threats in Punjab, Kashmir and the Northeast. Alongside dealing with continued ethno-national threats to it's territorial integrity over the last two decades, the very core of India's secular nationalist credentials has come to be questioned by the rise of the majoritarian Hindu nationalist movement.

Formed on the basis of a homeland for Muslims in the subcontinent, Pakistan's history has also been replete with movements of ethnic and religious resurgence. Averting early threats to it's territorial integrity from the Pashtun and the Baluch movements, it failed to adequately deal with the linguistic nationalist sentiments that emerged in East Pakistan (Phadnis & Ganguly, 2001: 11-12). In 1971, the success of the Bangladeshi independence movement convincingly put paid to the idea that a common religion was in itself sufficient in securing Pakistan's national unity. While ethnic strife remains a serious problem in Pakistan, ironically the most critical social fault-line has grown out of its very *raison-d'etat*. The spread of Muslim fundamentalist groups especially since the time of Zia has left Pakistani society deeply divided in defining Islam's role in the state.

While Bangladesh emphasised secularism in its national ideology at the time of independence, an Islamic revival emerged soon after the fall of the Mujib regime in 1975. Constitutional amendments that followed have come to reify the position of Islam in the young nation. The entrenchment of Islamic ideologies in the mainstream of Bangladeshi politics and the proliferation of fundamentalist institutions remains a matter of deep concern especially for the considerable Hindu minority in the state (Ahamed & Nazneen, 1990: 795). Although ethnic nationalism poses a secondary challenge in Bangladesh, given that it is the most ethnically homogeneous of the larger states in South Asia, attempts at assimilating the Hill Peoples of the Chittagong Hill Tracts into the dominant national identity of the state continue to be resisted.

This Volume

For the scholar of South Asian nationalisms, the revival of ethnic and religious identities poses a number of questions: To what extent can the answers to this 'primordial' resurgence be found in the political and socio-economic changes that have taken place in the modern state? Can the rise of these movements be attributed to a lack of power-sharing, or is it the case that these have emerged precisely as a result of an "increasingly consociational character" (Wilkinson, 2004:150)? What are the key elements of the political programme of these ethnic and religious groups and what effects do they have in reshaping the national ideology of the erstwhile state? Through an exposition of specific nationalist movements and ideology, the chapters in this volume seek to address some of these questions. Collectively they endeavour to provide, an account of why nationalism remains the single most critical factor shaping political developments in South Asia.

In 'Female Warriors, Martyrs and Suicide Attackers: Women in the LTTE', Dagmar Helmann-Rajanayagam elucidates on the divergent motives for the participation of Sri Lankan Tamil women in the Liberation Tigers of Tamil Eelam (LTTE). Charting the position of women in traditional Tamil society through an overview of classical Tamil literature, Helmann-Rajanayagam points out that warrior goddesses cannot account for female militancy since these deities were not perceived as suitable role models for women in Tamil society. Outlining the development of the LTTE, the author details the changes in LTTE propaganda, which increasingly reflected a desire to further the goal of women's emancipation. These changes, she posits, were tied to the LTTE's effort to increase the number of female recruits from the late 1970s. The cornerstone of Helmann-Rajanayam's chapter is the challenge she poses to scholars who attribute similar motives to the phenomenon of women suicide bombers in spite of differences in the nature of movements. She stresses that as far as women suicide bombers in LTTE are concerned, their motivations are predominantly national and not religious. Her ethnographic study further illustrates that the motives for female militancy have changed over time. While in the early 1980s a crucial factor were concerns to pre-empt rape by Sinhalese militia, in the late 1980s their motivations included, amongst others, the efficacy of the LTTE's propaganda in addressing women's concerns. Over the last decade, she notes that the reasons for female militancy have become more diverse, with some choosing to participate for adventure, to escape a problematic situation in the family, or to allow a brother to continue his studies in the context of the LTTE's call for the involvement of one child in every family. Helmann-Rajanayam's chapter goes on to address the resonance of women's participation in the LTTE on the wider issue of women's emancipation Sri Lankan Tamil society.

Shapan Adnan's chapter details the struggle of the indigenous people of the Chittagong Hill Tracts (CHT) of Bangladesh in the face of state-supported ethnic domination. Adnan unravels the deteriorating political, social and economic conditions of the Hill peoples by contrasting their position under successive regimes. He notes that while the indigenous people of the CHT were given special protection under British colonial rule, their position grew increasingly vulnerable following the region's incorporation into the Pakistani state in 1947. Developmental efforts, such the Kaptai Hydro-Electricity Project, did little for the Hill peoples, submerging large portions of their cultivable land and forcing thousands to flee to neighbouring India and Myanmar. Focusing on the debilitating situation of the Hill peoples following Bangladeshi independence in 1971, Adnan observes how in the face of pressure to assimilate into a hegemonic Bengali identity under Mujibur Rahman, the indigenous people of the CHT responded by setting up their own political party, the *Parbatya Chattagram Jana Samhati Samiti* (PCJSS), and forming a military wing, the *Shanti Bahini*. The unyielding stance of General Zia aggravated the crisis as the Hill peoples who were further subjected to a demographic engineering project that forced them out of their lands. Adnan's piece goes on to dissect the expansion of state interposition on issues of identity, nationalism and citizenship among the Hill peoples. Facing annihilation of their identity and habitat, he posits that the crystallization of a *Jumma* identity projected by the PCJSS for the Hill peoples came to be marked by a reaction to Bangladeshi nationalism, which sought to underplay differences within the ethnic groups that make up the indigenous people of the CHT.

Ishtiaq Ahmed's essay charts the historical changes in Pakistan's national identity. Ahmed points out that although Pakistan was formed on the premise of an exclusive cultural/ethnic type of nationalism based on the demand for separate statehood for Muslims, soon after independence in August 1947, Muhammad Ali Jinnah instead spoke of the need to establish an inclusive territorial nation that promised equal rights for all citizens. In the context of large-scale inter-religious violence manifest during the Partition, and the very fact that the Jinnah-led Muslim League had invoked Islam to mobilize support for a separate Pakistan, the author underscores that this inclusive vision of nationhood was untenable. While the role that Islam would play in the new state remained ambiguous and problematic for the Westernized Pakistani leaders, Ahmed reveals how gradually the position of Islam in the state comes to be entrenched and increasingly acquires fundamentalist trappings. The author meticulously details the measures taken by the Zia regime, supported by fundamentalists who had thus far remained at the periphery of political power, in accelerating the drive towards Islamisation through successive legislative changes that extended the reach of decrepit laws to cover diverse sections of society, including women, non-Muslims and minority sects. While the author acknowledges the September 11 attacks on the United States as a turning point in impeding the drive towards Islamisation, he points out that at best, the Musharraf regime was only able to vacillate between a moderate and fundamentalist type of Islam that on the one hand earned the ire of fundamentalists, while on the other leaving Pakistani women, non-Muslims and 'deviant' sects remaining subject to considerable disadvantage.

In her chapter 'The Khalistan movement in India: The interplay of politics and state power', Rajshree Jetly examines the growth of nationalist sentiment amongst Sikhs in the Indian state of Punjab from the 1980s. Jetly posits that the success or failure of Sikh demands for a separate homeland were closely tied to three contingencies–the nature of the movement, the response of the Central government, and the level of external support that the movement received. Jetly frames Sikh grievances in postcolonial India, underscoring the role of the political struggle between the Congress and the Akali Dal in fostering the growth of a demand for greater autonomy for the state. In explaining the rise of nationalist sentiment, the author emphasizes that economic grievances such as the lack of industrial development in the state were subsidiary to political issues, a growth of religious identification and a hard-line posture employed by the central government. The popularity of the movement however remained limited until the assault on the Golden Temple and the attacks of Sikhs which followed the assassination of Indira Gandhi in 1984. These tragic events effectively transformed the conflict to a full-blown separatist movement, drawing support from a wide range of Sikh communities both in the Punjab and in the diaspora. Reflecting on the decline of the movement by the early 1990s, Jetly opines that significant factors included the Centre's success in adopting a mix of force and conciliation, the alienation of ordinary people from the militants as a result of the atrocities committed by the latter, and the decline in external support both from Pakistan and amongst diasporic Sikhs.

Mahmoud Kashefi's thought provoking essay draws on sociological theories of revolution to scrupulously analyse the various phases of the Iranian Revolution in 1979. The potency of the article lies in the well thought out explanation it provides as to why the outcomes of the revolution varied so considerably from the initial demands of it's protagonists. In his study of the preconditions to the revolution, Kashefi reveals that none of the dissenting groups to Shah's rule, whether the modern middle class, the merchant capitalists (*bazaaries*), the working class or minority communities such as the Azerbaijanis, Arabs or Kurds sought a theocratic state. In all cases, their demands were either socio-political, i.e. calling for greater democracy, freedom and civil rights, or the result of economic grievances. He acknowledges, however, that the *bazaaries*, who were negatively affected by the advent of modern economic organizations under the Shah, were nonetheless allied to religious leaders. In his analysis of the second phase of the movement which concerns organizational leadership, Kashefi illustrates how secular socio-political groups that reflected the demands of the modern middle class such as the National Front and the Freedom Movement were unable to draw support from the lower classes. On the other hand the Left, which sought an all-out social revolution, was subject to brutal suppression by the Shah's forces, while at the same time being unable to fully command the working class who felt culturally alienated from it's political language that drew from various strands of Marxism. In this context, Kashefi notes, it was Khomeini's leadership that emerged as the most popular alternative. The author however strongly contends that rather than a call for theocratic state, it was Khomeni's populism, promising freedom and the end of foreign domination, which resulted in broad-based support. Reflecting on the outcomes of the revolution, the author underscores how Islamic fundamentalism in Iran has resulted in the betrayal and suppression of the very groups who were the mainstay of the revolution–the modern middle class and the working class-even as a mafia type economy has emerged whose main beneficiaries comprise religious leaders and the *bazaaries*.

Note

1. The term South Asia is often employed to refer to the member states of the South Asian Association for Regional Cooperation (SAARC) comprising India, Pakistan, Bangladesh, Sri Lanka, Afghanistan, Nepal, Maldives and Bhutan. Iran, though geographically located in Southern Asia has usually been defined as part of Southwestern Asia. In 2007, however, Iran sought and gained observer status in SAARC. This volume has adopted a more inclusive definition of South Asia that includes Iran, especially given its geographical proximity and it's strong historical ties with the member states of SAARC.

References

Ahamed, Emajuddin & Nazneed D. R. J. A. (1990). 'Islam in Bangladesh: Revivalism or Power Politics', *Asian Survey*, Vol. 30, No. 8, pp. 795-808.

Ahmed, Ishtiaq (2002). 'The 1947 Partition of India: A Paradigm for Pathological Politics in India and Pakistan', *Asian Ethnicity*, Vol. 3., no. 1, pp. 9-28.

Anderson, Benedict (1991). *Imagined Communities: Reflections on the Origin and Spread of Nationalism*, rev. edn., London: Verso.

Breuilly, John (1985). *Nationalism and the State*, rev. edn., Manchester: Manchester University Press.

Breuilly, John (1996). 'Approaches to Nationalism', in Balakrishna (ed.) *Mapping the Nation*, London: Verso, pp. 146-74.

Breuilly, John (2001). 'The State and Nationalism', in Guibernau, M. & Hutchinson, J. (eds.) *Understanding Nationalism*, Cambridge: Polity Press, pp. 32-52.

Connor, Walker (1994). *Ethnonationalism: The Quest for Understanding*, Princeton: Princeton University Press.

Dawisha, Adeed (2002). 'Nation and Nationalism: Historical Antecedents to Contemporary Debates', *International Studies Review*, Vol. 4, No. 1, pp. 3-22.

Gellner, Ernest (1983). *Nations and Nationalism*, Oxford: Billing and Sons.

Harrison, Selig S. (1960). *India: The Most Dangerous Decades*, Princeton: Princeton University Press.

Kellas, J. G. (1991). *The Politics of Nationalism and Ethnicity*, Basingstoke: Macmillan.

Munch, Ronaldo (1986). *The Difficult Dialogue: Marxism and Nationalism,* London: Zed Books.

Pieterse, J. N. (1997). 'Deconstructing/reconstructing Ethnicity', *Nations and Nationalisms,* Vol. 3, No. 3, pp. 365-95.

Phadnis, Urmila and Ganguly, Rajat (2001). *Ethnicity and Nation-building in South Asia,* rev. edn., New Delhi: Sage.

Romano, David (2006). *The Kurdish Nationalist Movement: Opportunity, Mobilization and Identity,* Cambridge, Cambridge University Press.

Sathyamurthy, T. V. (1998). 'Nationalism in the Era of Globalisation', *Economic and Political Weekly,* Vol. 33, No. 33/34, pp. 2247-52.

Smith, Anthony (1986). *The Ethnic Origins of Nations,* Oxford: Basil Biackwell.

Smith, Anthony (1996). 'Culture, Community and Territory: The Politics of Ethnicity and Nationalism', *International Affairs,* Vol. 72, No. 3, pp. 445-58.

Smith, Anthony (2000). 'Theories of Nationalism: Alternative Models of Nation Formation', in Leifer, Michael (eds.) *Asian Nationalism,* London: Routledge.

Tamir, Yael (1999). 'Theoretical Difficulties in the Study of Nationalism', in Beiner, Ronald (ed.) *Theorizing Nationalism,* New York: State University of New York Press, pp. 67-90.

Tonnesson, Stein & Antlov Hans, 'Asia in Theories of Nationalism and National Identity', in Tonnesson, Stein & Antlov Hans (eds.) *Asian Forms of the Nation,* Richmond: Curzon, pp.1-40.

United Nations (2006). *United Nations Member States, http://www.un.org/members/list.shtml* accessed on November 12, 2008.

Verdery, K. (1993). '"Whither" the "Nation" and "Nationalism"', *Daedalus,* Vol. 122, No. 3, pp. 37-46.

Wilkinson, Steven I. (2004). 'India, Consociational Theory and Ethnic Violence', in Varshney, Ashutosh (ed.) *India and the Politics of Developing Countries: Essays in Memory of Myron Weiner,* New Delhi: Sage, pp. 150-77.

Yack, Bernard (1999). 'The Myth of the Civic Nation', in Beiner, Ronald (ed.) *Theorizing Nationalism,* New York: State University of New York Press, pp. 103-118.

2

FEMALE WARRIORS, MARTYRS AND SUICIDE ATTACKERS: WOMEN IN THE LTTE*

DAGMAR HELLMANN-RAJANAYAGAM

Introduction

On 28th November 2007 a Tamil woman handicapped by polio gained access to the vicinity of a minister in the cabinet of Sri Lankan President Mahinda Rajapakse and Leader of the EPDP (Eelam People's Democratic Party), Douglas Devananda and detonated a bomb she had reportedly hidden in her bra (*www.iht* 2007, *www.spiegel.de*). While she and some of her bodyguards died, the minister remained unharmed. This incident was the last in a long list of suicide attacks performed by female members of the LTTE, the Liberation Tigers of Tamil Eelam. Before that, on 25th April 2006, another woman pretending to be pregnant had blown herself up near Lt. Gen. Sarath Fonseka who was severely injured in the attack (*www.bbc.co.uk*).

* A preliminary version of this paper was presented at the Deutscher Orientalistentag at Freiburg, Germany, 24th to 28th September 2007. I thank my audience and colleagues for helpful comments and queries.

Female suicide bombers have become notorious in several Islamic movements. Women in the LTTE came on the scene earlier (though they were not the first female suicide attackers), and have made their mark equally. The young woman who allegedly assassinated Rajiv Gandhi on 21st May 1991, Dhanu, is the most famous among them. The phenomenon of women suicide bombers has led several authors to lump all movements together and attribute the same or similar motives to all of them (Skaine, 2006: 85; Bloom, 2005: 11/86-88/99; Chenoy, 2002:18/19; Chenoy, 2004: 32/35).[1] This, however, is a misperception. For one thing, female fighters or female warriors are nothing new in various liberation movements the world over, at least in modern times, e.g. in Latin America, in the Spanish Civil War, the Communist Movement, the Italian Red Brigades in Italy and the Red Army Faction in Germany, and not least Laila Khaled, the PFLP (People's Front for the Liberation of Palestine) member, who became famous in the 1970s. What is astonishing is that again in modern times this fact should have attracted attention as something out of the ordinary, something not fit for women. Women, as Sandra Whitworth (2006: 125/26) and others have pointed out, are considered the opposite of fighters and warriors *by nature,* a species or group that need special persuasion or inducement to become violent (Coomaraswamy, 2002: 97). Chenoy (2002: 20) and Mukta (2004: 163-178; de Mel, 2001:209) among others, have argued that this is not the case. Especially in the Indian context, examples of fighting women and warrior goddesses abound (e.g., the Rani of Jhansi or Amba of the Mahabharata, or, nearer to our time, the women of the Indian National Army [Gopinath and Shivadas, 2007; Ward Fay 1991: 33]). The phenomenon of female suicide attackers, however, is more recent.

In this article, I shall undertake two things. First I will outline the concept of women's nature and roles in traditional and contemporary Tamil society in Sri Lanka. Since I have done this in detail in earlier pieces, I shall keep this short. Second, I shall introduce the LTTE, its history, programme, ideas and way of governing in the areas under its control and mainly outline related developments since 2002, as prior developments have been more extensively documented in Hellmann-Rajanayagam (1994; 2007a). In this context, I will emphasize the LTTE's concept of women and female warriors in greater detail, followed by some case descriptions.

The Concept of Woman in Tamil Society

Women in Tamil society in general have a respected but simultaneously ambivalent and somewhat restricted status. Early Tamil classical literature knows educated women in the shape of poetesses like Auvaiyar of the Puṟanāṉūṟu and in later centuries *devadasis* (temple dancers), like Madhavi of Cilappatikaram fame (1978). Queens are mentioned in the literature and in inscriptions by name as socially and economically powerful in their own right. The Tirukkural mentions the wife as the helpmate of her husband and on a more or less equal footing with him. Epics and folk tales from the later pre-colonial centuries, however, portray women as ideally weak, chaste, shut up in the home and ignorant about the outside world, and shy (Beck, 1982).[2] In these same tales, however, women have or acquire special powers as women, especially as married women and are labelled as the saviouresses of their menfolk (Viswanathan-Peterson, 1998). Folk wisdom and proverbs particularly in Northern Sri Lanka forbade education for women, and corporeal punishment of wives (though never of the honoured mother, who was a temple) was considered an honourable act (Hellmann-Rajanayagam, 2007a: 159).[3]

In any case, like in many traditional societies, women could gain social standing primarily as wives and mothers of sons, even though the famed poetesses were thought to have been unmarried. In spite of this very restrictive attitude education of women and girls was introduced in Jaffna quite early: with the foundation of the first girls' school in Vattukkottai by the American Mission in 1823. This school became extremely successful in a short time, because even traditional Jaffna recognised the value of education for women. The most well-known religious reformer[4] of Jaffna, Arumuka

Navalar (Hellmann-Rajanayagam, 1989), argued for the education of girls already in the 1850s, because, he said, only then would they become good wives and mothers and would be able to conduct the affairs of their husbands in an emergency (Hellmann-Rajanayagam, 2007a: 158/59). The Sinhalese areas traditionally granted more freedom to women, yet it took much longer for girls' schools to get accepted there.

Whereas classical Tamil literature and mythology do know warrior goddesses like Durga, the slayer of demons and Kali, the goddess of war and of the cremation ground (to name only a few), neither heroic literature nor reality give us any hint about female fighters or warriors: men fight and women induce them to it (Puṟanāṉūṟu 276, 277, 279; Trawick, 1999: 158/59; de Mel 2004: 77). The goddesses are, however, not considered role models for women, they are wild and dangerous virgins; rather the married and thus tamed goddesses like Lakshmi and Parvati are emulated (Hellmann-Rajanayagam/Fleschenberg, 2008). We do not, e.g. find a figure like the Rani of Jhansi.

The LTTE–A Short Outline

Let us briefly look at the LTTE, the Liberation Tigers of Tamil Eelam or Tamil Tigers for short (Hellmann-Rajanayagam 1994, 2007a: 485ff). The movement was established in 1976 and originated out of several student wings of the respective Tamil parties in the North and Northeast of Sri Lanka. The militant movements–and there were far more than one–were dissatisfied with the slow and hesitant progress of the established parties to achieve justice and equal treatment for the Tamils in Sri Lanka. While the parent parties relied–unsuccessfully–on parliamentary methods, the youth came to believe that only militant methods would ensure that the Tamils would no longer be treated as second-class citizens in their own country as had been the case for decades after independence. If the long-standing demand for autonomy would not serve, why not ask for an independent Tamil state straight away? This had been the election demand of the Tamil coalition TULF (Tamil United Liberation Front, established in

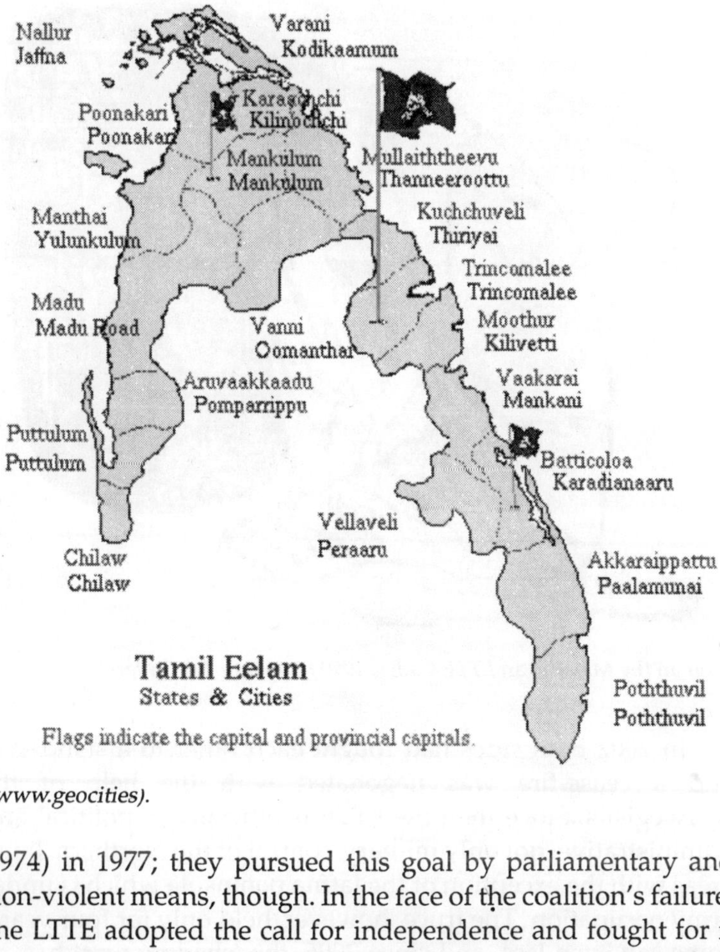

(www.geocities).

1974) in 1977; they pursued this goal by parliamentary and non-violent means, though. In the face of the coalition's failure, the LTTE adopted the call for independence and fought for it since 1983 in a bloody and brutal war with the Sri Lankan Armed Forces. Fortunes repeatedly changed for both sides. Suicide attacks and assassinations were means of choice for the Tigers, at least as long as they conducted a guerrilla war. In later years they fought increasingly conventional campaigns, complemented by daring attacks on military and economic targets. The Sri Lankan armed forces, in turn, employed arbitrary arrests, harsh anti-terror laws (which created the terrorists they were aimed to eradicate), rape and torture, all to no avail.

Woman (by Malathi, an LTTE Cadre, 1990 (Sathyam Art Gallery)

In 2002 both sides had fought each other to a stand-still, and a cease-fire was negotiated with the help of the Norwegians. Since then the LTTE is officially in political and administrative, not only military, control of the Northern Tamil areas with the exception of the Jaffna peninsula which is under army occupation. The truce, however, held only for four years, some say even less, and since 2006, the 'shadow war' has, as admitted by both sides, turned into full-fledged war again. The Sri Lanka Government officially annulled the agreement on 2nd January 2007 (*www.tamilnet.com* 2008). A renewed offensive by the Sri Lankan Armed Forces in the North, announced since the summer of 2007, when it had purportedly regained the East, has not really got off the ground, partly because of fierce resistance by the LTTE, partly because of second thoughts by the Sinhalese. The situation has turned into the usual stale-mate, well-known since two decades.

Women in the LTTE

To what extent did the LTTE take into account or further feminist aspirations or 'women's concerns'? Like other militant groups among the Tamils and in Sri Lanka in general, the LTTE propagated equal rights and treatment for women from the start in its writings and propaganda statements. But it was one of the first militant groups to go beyond that and to actively call and recruit women into the movement as active members and fighters from the late 70s and early 80s onwards. The argument was that only in this way would it be possible to further and ensure women's emancipation.

This was a radical step, and it may be compared with the situation in some Islamic countries. As stated above, women had traditionally been relegated to the domestic sphere in Tamil Sri Lanka and active female warriors were quite unknown. The TULF, while politically radical in its demands for an independent Tamil state, showed a strange restraint where women's questions were concerned and rarely recruited women even for political work. In the early 20th century, voting rights for women had been fiercely opposed by the conservative elite of Jaffna, led by the politician P. Ramanathan, and when universal suffrage was granted to Sri Lanka in 1931, this meant the end of the world as he knew it for him (Hellmann-Rajanayagam, 2007a: 50/51). Very few Tamil women were active in the Ceylonese parties and the struggle for independence, whatever little there was of it (Jayawardena/Kodikara, 2002: 433).[5] On the Sinhala side, this looked different: here women did get involved in the demand for independence and in political work (Jayawardene, 2000; 2005). But compared with the activities of women in India this remained on a very modest scale. The percentage of women in parliament stagnated around 4% for decades (Jayawardena/Kodikara, 2002: 432; Goonesekere, 2002).[6] This did not change even when Sirima Bandaranaike became the successor of her husband after the latter's assassination. She was more an exception than a role model.

The LTTE, when it gradually turned into the only militant organisation that had any weight in the Tamil areas in the 80s and could spread its ideas in the North, first rather unthinkingly and naively demanded 'emancipation of women' without clearly spelling out what this might mean under the circumstances. It seems to have been a slogan rather than a programme that was part of the propaganda of a credible militant movement, particularly, since all other militant organisations spouted the same phrases. There was little consideration of actual social and political conditions and traditions. Demands and accusations remained generalised and insufficiently took into account the actual social situation in Jaffna. They originated from a vaguely leftist and socialist attitude, influenced to a not inconsiderable extent by corresponding developments among the Sinhalese, especially in the JVP. Here, too, 'emancipation of women' was part of the baggage without its contents being always clearly spelt out.

An example for the confusion would be the demand for the abolition of the 'dowry evil', no doubt taken from similar demands in India. The 'dowry evil' is certainly one such in India and has justly attracted attention and opprobrium not only from women's organisations and movements. Dowry is interdicted by law there. The topic was unquestioningly adopted in Sri Lanka without considering the rather different situation there.[7] Adele Balasingham (1993) authored besides her portrayal of female fighters in the LTTE a pamphlet entitled 'unbroken chains', that described the dire situation of women in Jaffna and the alleged dowry evil–without wasting a word of explanation on the original meaning and legal constitution of dowry in traditional Jaffna society (Balasingham, 1994). According to the Tecavalamai, the traditional law of Jaffna, dowry was given to daughters in lieu of inheritance, because they were not entitled to inherit. The brothers in a family were not able to marry before they had earned the dowries for all their sisters. This dowry was intended to ensure that the daughter and wife was economically secure even if the husband died or left her. It was only inheritable in the female line: from mother to daughter or granddaughter, or to the niece and grandniece. If the wife died without issue, it fell back to her mother or other female relatives (Mutukistna, 1862). The husband could manage his wife's property only with her consent. Only in 1911 the British administration changed this by law and enabled the husband to dispose of his wife's property without her consent (Hellmann-Rajanayagam 2007a: 222; 1994: 69/70; Thambiah 1950). There is no doubt that after this legislation dowry really became an 'evil' and now considerably limits the marriage prospects of many girls in Jaffna (CaImukaliEkaI, 2002).

Which is why the LTTE forbade it while administering Jaffna and forbids or at least discourages it nowadays in Killinochi, on pain of severe penalties. Adele Balasingham (1998: 299f) has considerably changed her view of dowry in later publications. But even in her study 'Will to Freedom' she laments the fate of Tamil women who are only allowed to be wives and mothers and demarcates herself from them explicitly– simultaneously and by her own admission profiting from the help and care of precisely these wives and mothers.

The image of woman in the LTTE changed only very gradually and with a growing number of female members. At the same time, demands and programmes became more specific. Nowadays it is not so much the dowry that is considered evil, but how it is demanded and used (see below). A similar change has occurred with the attitude towards rape. In the 80s, when brutal rapes of Tamil women and girls by Sinhalese soldiers were wide-spread (they still are common) and feared, the LTTE condemned these incidents with the explicit argument that the violated women were not longer fit to marry Tamil men (Hellmann-Rajanayagam, 1986: 75; de Mel, 2001: 212).[8] The alleged sexual impurity and loss of chastity were the only factors considered important, not the violation of the physical integrity of the woman. This led to severe criticism of the *machismo* of the LTTE. But it was only when a women's wing of the LTTE was established that the argument of shame and impurity gradually faded into the background. Nowadays rape is still little talked about, but this is a conscious policy of the women's organisations: rape should not be made into a political instrument as has been the case in Bosnia (Trawick 1990).[9] Women who are raped are told in consultation that this is nothing to be ashamed of, it should be considered on the level of an accident for which the woman could not be blamed (Yo. Kalaivilly, 2004). The LTTE encourages its veterans to marry women who have been raped to ensure their social standing.

Rape, (by K.Rajah (Sathyam Art Gallery)

Women Fighters of the LTTE

Under the conditions described the recruitment of women for combat was not really easy. Only the efforts of Lt. Col. Tilipan, a high-ranking LTTE-member, bore fruit in the 80s. Tilipan (Rasiah Parthipan) was a third-year medical student from Urelu and student leader who joined the LTTE in 1983 and quickly became first its propagandist and then Political Head of Jaffna. In 1987 he fasted to death in protest against the actions (or rather lack action) of the IPKF in Jaffna and violations of the ceasefire (*www.ltteps*). He focussed on recruiting young women for the movement.

Today it is assumed that between 30-40% of LTTE fighters are women who are organised in separate women's regiments under female leadership. In the suicide cadres, the number of men and women are said to be equal (though this is questionable:

in the lists of martyrs given out every year on Heroes' Day, there are still far fewer women listed than men).

Warrior Painter Neethan's 'Colours of the Dawn' (Sathyam Art Gallery)

Individual reasons for joining the LTTE varied considerably. In the early 80s women became members of the LTTE (and other militant organisations) to escape or pre-empt rape by Sinhalese or Indian soldiers. Others joined precisely because they had been raped. This led to the claim that rape was the only reason for women to join a militant movement or become a suicide bomber (de Mel, 2004: 75/84/85).[10] This, however, appears to be an oversimplification. Rape might have been a reason to join or turn into a suicide bomber in some cases, but not the major one. Besides, when the character of the armed struggle and the organisation changed in the late 80s and 90s from a guerrilla group to a virtually conventional force, women's motivations to join the organisation also changed. They currently cover a wide spectrum: the efficiency and appeal of LTTE propaganda to come to the aid of the motherland made young women want to be part of the movement; yet equally frequently it was the experience of violent attacks by the Sri Lankan Army, injury and death of near relatives and friends that induced them to violent struggle. One young student told:

> In 1997 the Sri Lankan Army flew a bomb attack on the school I was attending. We ran into the jungle and some of my class mates and teachers died. The next day most of our class went to the LTTE camp to join. I was 16 at the time. Unfortunately they rejected me as too small and weak. They told me to go on studying and then work for the country in some other way (personal communication 2007).

In many cases, however, particularly in the 90s and after 2002, it was simply the desire for adventure or to do something 'cool' which all her peers were doing as well that made young, sometimes underage, girls to show up as recruits in the LTTE camps. In more serious cases they sometimes tried to escape a family situation that had become unbearable: either because of an alcoholic, abusive father, extreme poverty or the threat to be forced into marriage with somebody they did not like. A member of the SLMM, the Sri Lanka Monitoring Mission who was in charge of returning underage LTTE members to their families, told me that sometimes she did this with a heavy heart, since the family situation was not such that she would willingly expose them again to a broken home. Most of these children, however, or so she said, came from quite good and intact families, but thought it the 'in thing' to join the LTTE, since all their friends did the same. We agreed that it could be compared to the fashion of body piercing in Europe, which induces similar horror in parents (personal communication 2003). Frequently it is impossible to tell why a particular woman joined the movement, and general explanations cannot be given. Most women I talked to cited the experience of oppression by the Sinhalese armed forces or the persuasive power of LTTE leader V. Prabhakaran's speeches. Some followed the call to arms in order to enable an elder or younger brother to study. This was at the time when the LTTE asked for one child of each family to join the movement.

With the growing power of the LTTE female fighters have become increasingly visible. They have remained easily identifiable in public life after the ceasefire due to their distinctive 'civil uniform': loose dark trousers, a long men's shirt in sober colours tightly belted and short hair or long plaits wound tightly round the head. Nothing could be more different from the traditional dress of Tamil women and girls: the sari or long skirt and blouse and long plaits or a bun adorned with flowers. Only when they leave the movement to return to civil life do they revert to more or less traditional clothes: long skirts, shalwar kameez or jeans and shirts. Former female fighters are seldom seen in saris, except for functions or in the temple. The dressing habits are a clear political statement and they give the lie to rumours that made the rounds in the 80s and early 90s, that the LTTE had put out a leaflet to force women to wear only saris on pain of severe punishment (de Mel 2001: 216).[11]

As soon as the first female fighters fell victim to armed battle, they were given the status and title of *Mavirar,* as was done for their male comrades. The term may be translated as Great Hero, it is, however, mostly rendered as 'martyr' by the LTTE. And thus we come to the female martyrs.

Female Martyrs

The first to be granted this title was 2nd Lt. Malathy (Malthi, Malathi) from Mannar. She is honoured by statues and monuments in Killinochi and the day of her death has become Tamil Eelam Women's Awakening Day (*www.tamilnet.com* a). Her real–Catholic-name was Cakayacili Peturuppillai. She

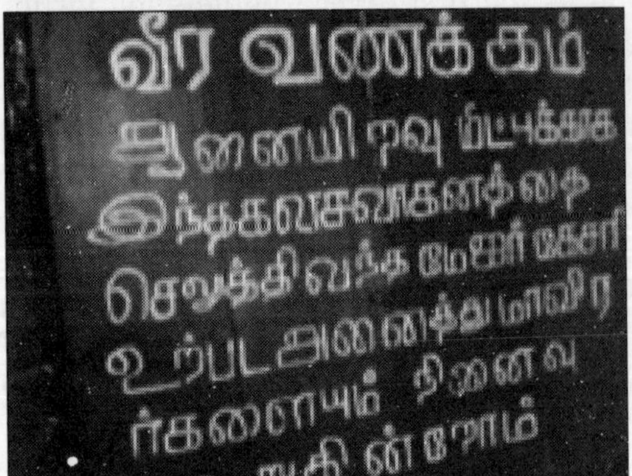
வீர வணக்கம்

died on 10th October 1987 at the age of twenty in a battle between the LTTE and the IPKF at Kopay by her own hand. Her comrade Janani told how she was wounded in both legs and could not escape, so she sent the other women away and took cyanide (Balasingham, www.tamilnation). Malathy was only the first in a long line of women martyrs of the LTTE like Major Kecari who died in the attack at Elephant Pass. The first and the early martyrs commonly attain a particularly high status. Brigades and Regiments are named after them. Unfortunately, none of the eloges and articles on Malathy tell us anything about her reasons to join the LTTE or about her biography. She seems to have come on the scene like Aphrodite, born of foam. On the other hand, every year on her memorial day, it is reported that her parents publicly garland her tomb stone and her statue (*www.tamilnet* b).

On another level altogether is Annai Pupati (Mother Pupati). Her full name was Kanapatipillai Pupati, and she died in a temple in Batticaloa on 19th April 1988 at the age of 56–after refusing both food and fluids for 30 days. She seems, according to all accounts, to have been a very inconspicuous, traditional Tamil woman, married at twelve and widowed soon after. She remarried a widower with three children, something not totally unheard of in Jaffna, and had altogether ten children. She turned radical after two of her sons had been killed by the army and a third been arrested and tortured in Boosa camp. She became a member of the Mothers' Front in Navatkeni, a women's group who non-violently protested against the army occupation and violation of human rights and enquired after the fate of 'disappeared' Tamil youth in army and police camps. On 19th March 1988 she commenced her fast unto death in protest against the actions of the IPKF and to demand a ceasefire and negotiations between the combatants (*www.tamilnation.org* a). She is honoured by special ceremonies every year in the Northeast and in Jaffna.

I have dealt with the question of martyrs and gender differences in the evaluation of martyrs in another place and shall therefore only briefly discuss the question here (Hellmann-Rajanayagam, 2008 a). To put it shortly, men become pure by dying a martyr's death, women retain their purity. While this applies particularly to the Indian cultural area, the same concept is not unknown even in the Christian tradition. In India, this becomes especially clear in the concept of the Sati who immolates herself after her husband's death on his funeral pyre. For *satis,* occasionally hero or memorial stones were erected like for a fallen warrior. This statement is, however, problematic within the context of LTTE ideology, since it demands chastity (*karpu*) from both sexes. *Karpu* is here understood less as virginity and/or sexual purity, than as (sexual) self-control and restraint (Schalk, 1994: 178; Viswanathan-Peterson, 1998: 41).[12] As a secular movement (that is how it portrays and presents itself quite aggressively in public) it strictly rejects the concept and practice of Sati. Female and male martyrs are honoured in exactly the same way: through monuments, memorial stones and statues and anniversary celebrations on the day of their death each year.

Suicide Bombers

Suicide assassins (*karumpuli*), though labelled and honoured as martyrs (*mavirar*) by the LTTE and often equated in the media, particularly when dealing with Islamic violence, must be distinguished from the latter. All fighters who fall in battle or during special actions, are martyrs. Thus, suicide attackers count as martyrs as a matter of course, but they belong in another category. Only occasionally named monuments are erected for them, and in many cases, suicide attackers remain anonymous. Named monuments exist, like for normal martyrs, for the first suicide tigers, Sivakumaran and Capt. Miller. The most well-known suicide bomber, however, never got a monument: Dhanu, who allegedly assassinated Rajiv Gandhi (Sarvan, 1998: 357-361).[13] Officially, the LTTE has never acknowledged her as one of their own. Suicide bombers or, to give them their proper name, Black Tigers are selected and trained specially (Hellmann-Rajanayagam, 2007). They apply of their own volition, but very few are chosen. They are taught to consider their lives as weapon and as a special gift:

tankotai,[14] which they donate for a higher goal, viz. the liberation of the Tamil Motherland. Reason and goal of dying are national, not religious ones, whether for men or for women (Hellmann-Rajanayagam, 2005). It is important to emphasise this point: moral or religious reasons are never adduced for suicide attacks, we find no idea of *karma,* of rebirth or entry into a paradise. The only reward for a black Tiger is the idea of contributing to the liberation of the motherland. This is a decisive and conspicuous difference to the ideals current in Islamic militant movements (Victor, 2003).

Ideals and Role Models

Before discussing the question of women's emancipation or 'empowerment' through militancy, it will be instructive to investigate to which ideals or role models the LTTE harks back in its efforts to bring women into the organisation. For the struggle in general and its support by women classical heroic literature is consciously, albeit, selectively, chosen. The Pu<u>r</u>anā<u>n</u>ū<u>r</u>u (278; 277) furnishes enough blood-soaked examples for this kind of event.[15] But classical literature cannot be used to justify the recruitment of women nor can religious models be applied. Active combat by women is not sanctioned by tradition and is indeed considered and propagated as something new and somehow a break with the past. Instead, the Indian freedom struggle provides suitable examples to follow. This applies both to the struggle led by Gandhi and the Indian National Congress and–even more–to the movement led by Subhas Chandra Bose and the Indian National Army. The INA is the Indian organisation on which the LTTE consciously wants to model itself, and this applies also to its treatment and employment of women. The INA contained a very active women's regiment, the Rani of Jhansi regiment which was led by Lakshmi Sahgal, née Swaminathan, a Tamil doctor from Malaya. She drew numerous Tamil women into the INA, among them Bupalan Rasammah (Gawankar, 2003: 91f; Ward Fay, 1995: 33). This regiment gave women for the first time, according to their own statements, a feeling of being humans and not redundant and superfluous chattels. Similar statements we have from Tamil men from Malaya as well, who gave this as a reason to join the

INA: they were for the first time in their lives treated as human beings.

Woman Fighters: Empowerment?

The significance of female militancy for women's emancipation is fiercely debated. To set the scene for the discussion, I describe here several of my 'encounters with tigresses':

(1) Shortly after the ceasefire agreement in February 2002 I could, after a long interruption, again travel to the Tamil areas. LTTE cadres were conducting me to the town of Mullaittivu when our jeep's axle broke roughly half-way. Until a new vehicle could be organised, I was conveyed (a rather highflown term for a bumpy journey riding pillion on the motorcycle of the camp commander into the interior of scrub jungle) to a women's camp near Utaiyarkadu The commander was 28-years old Lt. Col. Bhavaniti. She had fought in the battle of Elephant Pass in 2000-when the LTTE overran the Sri Lanka army base camp there and reconquered the pass with heavy casualties for the Sinhalese–and in Pallai some months later. She had commanded a battalion of 500 soldiers. She led the Kutti Sri Regiment[16] and had been a member of the LTTE since 1993. She explained that she had sustained hundred casualties, both dead and injured, in the various battles. In early 2003 the camp had been virtually closed down, only ten fighters were still administering it. Bhavaniti was extremely pleased by my visit and by the interest I took in the camp and in her personal story and insisted that I could not leave before I had had lunch with her. She came across as a very pleasant, self-assured young women with a natural authority. All women in the camp wore the typical uniform of the tigresses; only one girl was dressed in skirt and blouse on account of a landmine having torn of her calf. She told me that she was 21 years old and had taken part in battles for Elephant and in Chavakaccheri in 2001 (if this was the case, she

must have been recruited at an age of 18 or even 17). Bhavaniti hailed from Chavakaccheri where most of her family still lived. Some of her brothers and sisters had gone to live in Canada and Switzerland. She herself stayed in a pleasantly furnished little bungalow with floor and steps constructed from ammunition boxes on which one could still discern the writing 'Sri Lankan Armed Forces'. She was happy about the ceasefire, but ready to go into battle again for her leader and the country. Once peace came she would like to study computer science. Would she want to marry? Oh yes, surely, one day, but not yet. The entrance into the camp was strictly controlled not so much for reasons of security, but for those of propriety: only women could enter the *sanctus sanctorum,* the commander's bungalow. The young men accompanying me had to wait beyond the fence in the visitors' room which simultaneously functioned as a memorial room for the founder-martyr of the regiment: Kutti Sri. It was, as one of the SLMM-officers later put it, a rather monastic atmosphere with the commander as the mother Abbess. Not a bad comparison: both the atmosphere of dedication and the segregation of males and females reminded one of monastic conditions. The military training likewise is conducted in a strictly segregated manner, even though the trainers of the women cadres are sometimes still male fighters (Trawick, 1999: 145).[17]

(2) I had later occasion to meet Thamilini, the leader of the women's wing of the LTTE, and her assistants, several times on each of my subsequent visits between 2004 and 2007. Thamilini is a very bubbly and energetic young lady in her mid-thirties belonging to a Karaiyar family from the Vanni. The Karaiyar are the second-largest caste among the Sri Lankan Tamils, the highest and most numerous caste being the Vellalar. The Karaiyar are originally fisherpeople and for centuries furnished the military forces of the Jaffna

kings. They have a reputation of pride and ferocity. They do not fit easily in the caste hierarchy of Tamil Sri Lanka, since they consider themselves as standing and acting outside or alongside it (Pfaffenberger, 1982; Hellmann-Rajanayagam, 2007a; 135f; idem, 2004: 105). A large number of them are Catholics. Quite a number of the female fighters are, by their own statements, Karaiyar from very humble backgrounds (Kalaivilly, 2004). At the time of the first interview Thamilini had just finished a very active military career and had got involved in politics to the extent that she supported the election campaign of the female candidates of the TNA, the Tamil National Alliance, especially Pathmini Sithamparanathan. She also supported or was a member in several women's organisations and NGOs. She has, however, not left the LTTE yet. At the last meeting she stated matter-of-factly that she would probably have to take part in military operations again soon.

In Thamilini's view the war has provided a significant change of roles for women, this could, however, not be considered final. The gains of the war would have to be cemented in peace negotiations-if ever they would be resumed–through a new definition of the role of women and in legislation. A most interesting development in this regard was the close contacts and cooperation of the LTTE women's wing with the Social Scientists' Association in Colombo and one of its fellows, Kumari Jayewardene. These contacts were kept up long after the ceasefire had been suspended and many other contacts had broken down. Thamilini emphasised that she we was less interested in the abolition of dowry, but in its correct, i.e. traditional interpretation according to the *Tecavalamai*, whose regulations have been outlined above (Thamilini, 2004, 2004a, 2007).

(3) LTTE-women, who have left active service may remain in the movement or return to civil life. In the former case they may become members of the politbureau like Thamilini, work in the Peace Secretariat, like Selvy, its Human Rights spokeswoman, the PDS, like Gita, or the TRO, as principals of LTTE-children's homes, like Jayanani or, as was the case especially after the Tsunami, they work as doctors in the Tilipan Primary Health Centres and other health institutions with limited means but great dedication. 40% of Tamil Eelam Police personnel are women, and many health, education and administrative institutions are led and run by former LTTE women with great efficiency. LTTE women are marked off from the remainder of the female population not only by their dress and hair style, but much more by their demeanour and comportment. They spread an aura of determination and self-assurance which is not commonly shown by women in Sri Lanka publicly. Margaret Trawick (1999; 151), whose study is one of the first and most comprehensive ones about women members of the LTTE claims that the women fighters still follow old role patterns in interactions with men as well as with others of their own sex. Only during active fights,

which for them are a necessary task to be fulfilled as well as possible including the annihilation of the adversary, she says, they become different personalities (Trawick 1999: 155). While it is true that frequently traditional patterns of interaction are still enacted, especially in encounters with superiors, the self-confidence and self-assurance of LTTE women in all areas of daily life is visible: they would, e.g. never hesitate to move anywhere alone even at night, something unthinkable for even the most confident Tamil woman in Jaffna and Killinochi. While men would not dare to trifle with these women, they are nothing like their description in the Sinhalese media: dour, humourless fighting robots, but rather pleasant-spoken, merry and friendly young women, who treat the inquisitive visitor with great kindliness and courteous firmness.

Autonomy Through Militancy?

Can membership in a militant group at all have an emancipatory effect? The segregated training and fighting situation of the LTTE's regiments and the participation of women in suicide attacks have attracted reproaches that the LTTE's concern for women's liberation were dishonest and superficial and that it tried to recruit women merely since there were, for various reasons, not enough young men to join. Besides, sexual segregation and forced recruitment were no means to overcome women's disadvantages (Coomaraswamy, 2005).[18] It is not quite easy to follow these arguments if one at the same time considers another one often voiced (frequently by precisely the same commentators) that describes the LTTE as one of the most forceful and most committed militant movements existing. A movement that is able to generate a willingness for struggle and sacrifice to such an extent as the LTTE, without the prospects of future rewards or a glorious hereafter, would be hard put to it to use unlimited coercion to recruit new blood.

Sexual segregation may be (or may have been) a first step to get women on the same level as men (de Mel, 2001: 207/219;

Trawick 1999: 158).[19] A more grievous accusation has been that recruitment into militant organisations in order to exert violence cannot be a true move in the direction of women's liberation (de Cataldo-Neuburger/Valentini, 1996: 1-2). This argument proceeds from the above-mentioned assumption that women are by nature peaceful and virtually born for mediation, peace-building and healing. Within the specific context of Sri Lankan Tamil women Darini Rajasingham-Senanayake (2001: 117/121-124) and Adele Balasingham (1998: 279f) have, from widely diverging perspectives, shown that many of the women joining the LTTE feel autonomous and able to decide about their destiny for themselves for the first time in their lives. They retain this feeling and this attitude on their return to civil life. We earlier mentioned the same happening in the INA, when many Tamils felt for the first time acknowledged and treated as humans by a movement considered fascist and treasonable by the British.

A New Image of Woman?

Susanne Schröter has recently outlined the reasons why Muslim women might become suicide attackers (Schröter 2008, forthcoming). These reasons turn on social marginalisation and oppression or on perceived– sexual–shame and guilt as well as increasingly religious motivations. The latter is in contrast to the women, like Laila Khaled who played a prominent role in the militant Palestine movement in the 70s, and who were secular and autonomous. Secular and autonomous is also a fitting description of Tamil Tigresses (whether they are religious in private life or not): The LTTE does not recruit women to expiate some alleged disgrace, but to fight for the motherland. Suicide attacks are incidental, not, as in Islamic movements, an end in themselves. Tigresses do precisely not become *Satis* by other means. Even if sometimes their reasons for joining armed struggle derive from a difficult or broken family situation, they are not triggered by banishment from the family due to some alleged misdemeanour or wrong-doing. Surviving women fighters return to civil life, become professionals, marry and have children. But: they mostly choose their husbands themselves instead of bowing down to their parents' wishes. Some, like Thamilini and Bhavaniti, reject marriage for the time being, even though, as Kumari Jayawardene emphasises, familial pressure to marry is often very strong even for women Tigers: they have more important things to do and the taste of freedom is addictive. Participation in armed struggle involves overwhelmingly an element of voluntariness, much less despair about the hopelessness of personal circumstances.

To put it briefly, Tamil women join the Tigers not to die, but to fight. Death is taken into account, but is not necessarily anticipated. This is a decisive difference to the situation of Muslim women (de Mel, 2001: 220; Schröter, 2008; Victor, 2003).[20]

The problem for female LTTE-fighters lies elsewhere. It is twofold: on the one side a clear awareness of a tradition and social ideology disadvantageous to women that has been exacerbated by British legislation of the late 19th century. LTTE women want to re-establish freedoms granted them in pre-colonial times. On the other side-and Thamilini thinks this is far more serious–we see that female LTTE members are not really acknowledged as role models for most Tamil women in Sri Lanka: they are being admired, but they are not emulated. They seem to be predestined to do things for women that other women are not able or not prepared to achieve. Thamilini put it pithily: most women still cling to the KKK-ideal.[21] Moreover, there are reports that many families do not like to marry their sons to female Tigers (which is not really to be wondered at!).

Tigresses act, like the goddess, outside of a social structure handed down for centuries and thus, cannot be role models. Many women feel uncomfortable in the presence of tigresses, maybe because they feel inadequate themselves (or because they do not consider them real women?). Or it might be because many female fighters, like male ones belong in the Karaiyar caste. On the other hand some Tigresses seem to nurse slight contempt for the KKK-women who are trapped in out-dated ideas and anxieties. Yet these attitudes, Thamilini thinks, are the ones most difficult to overcome. The Tigresses thus perceive the problems of transition from a war to a peace culture very acutely, but they are still in the process of envisaging how to achieve this transition in a manner that is just and satisfactory for women.

So we come around again to the persistent question whether membership in radical groups can be liberating or not. It is impossible to decide on this question generally and finally, and the debate will probably rage for a long time to come. At the end, however, a somewhat uncomfortable observation: even in Germany, the rethinking of customary female roles only really began with 68ers' movement and the establishment of the violent Baader-Meinhof-group. Is then, to misquote Herodot, battle really the mother of all things?

Notes

1. Chenoy argues, that feminist argument of the 'naturally peaceful woman' is just the obverse of the male, patriarchal view that peaceful men are weak and feminised.
2. In the Cilappatikāram, however, only Kannaki is described as such. Her husband Kovalan's mistress Madhavi, is both educated and accomplished as well as independent and knowledgeable.
3. Though this might have less to do with the wife being a woman, but with the women being a wife: Indira Viswanathan-Peterson describes how in many folk tales the bond between brothers and sisters is the strongest love bond, where the wife only comes in as a necessary, but malignant and disturbing factor. This idea may be due to the Dravidian kinship system where close cousins are the ideal marriage partners.
4. Though reformer is a misnomer: Navalar put across an extremely traditional, one could say reactionary view of women and their role, which makes his advocacy for female education the more remarkable.
5. Between 1942 and 1980 there not one Tamil woman was a member of Parliament.
6. For years after independence, the figure varied between 1% and 3%.
7. In Tamilnadu, as well, the institution of dowry worked out rather differently from the North.

8. De Mel, while not denying the changes, claims that LTTE patriarchy claws back its power by redefining itself and throwing women back on their reproductive role. This might be true or not, but it is certainly unique: it has happened in Germany after WWII as well.
9. Margaret Trawick puts it more sharply: 'Women have now decided that talking about their problems will never put an end to their problems. They have to challenge.'
10. De Mel describes pointedly the dangers and the inadmissibility of linking these women's reasons for conducting suicide attacks exclusively to motivations of sexuality/sexual violation. Apart from anything else, it would deny her agency and personality. She speaks of about 64 known–because dead–female suicide cadres.
11. The reference for the quote is Sitralega Maunaguru in another study. This essay again quotes from another publication: I have not been able to trace the original of the quote anywhere and have a strong suspicion that it was either a fake or never existed.
12. Viswanathan-Peterson argues similarly, that *karpu* as 'learned inward control' is unrelated to marriage and denotes a source of sacred power.
13. Instead, she has acquired an eternal literal life elsewhere: in short stories and plays. All these suffer from the fact that none of the authors has ever met, let alone talked to, Dhanu in the flesh, and that they harp on the sexual angle. De Mel, who has written extensively about women suicide cadres has met and interviewed none of them, she relies on mediated interviews and reports of former LTTE women who have turned hostile to the movement. It seems that even after the cease-fire, with few exceptions, none of these authors ventured into the Tamil areas for a first-hand look and to take into account the changes the cease-fire had wrought.
14. This is a word play on the Tamil term for suicide: *tarkolai* = killing of self whereas *tankotai* is translated as gift of self.
15. "Greater joy than on the day I bore him I have today from my son." A mother on finding her son cut in four pieces on the battlefield.
16. Named after another martyr of the movement.

17. "It is Tiger policy for male and female combatants to treat one another with respectful distance."
18. This was the strongly voiced opinion of Radhika Coomaraswamy, former spezial UN-envoy for violence against women and children.
19. While de Mel laments the sexual containment and the corresponding emphasis on women's sexuality and its redirection towards militancy, she overlooks in this partly quite observant outline that the same 'eroticising of the martial' (p. 207) occurs in purely male movements and armies since time immemorial. At the least this segregation would prevent abuse of women as has (been alleged to have) happened in the US armed forces. Trawick puts the whole matter into a suitable perspective: "Such observations belie the rumours that members of the LTTE are either sexually repressed or promiscuous. I would suggest that investigations into the sexual life of the LTTE members will yield no exciting discoveries."
20. de Mel questions this. She considers the element of dutiful sacrifice and martyrdom overriding even for Tamil women. Here, as often elsewhere, there seems to be confusion and conflation of female fighters , suicide cadres, and martyrs.
21. A derogatory term employed by the feminist movement in Germany during the 70s and 80s: Kinder, Küche, Kirche = Children, Kitchen, Church. Thamilini has visited Germany several times and discussed with women's groups, so the term was familar to her. She used it with considerable amusement.

References

Balasingham, Adele (1998). Will to Freedom. An Inside View of Tamil Resistance London: Fairmax.

Balasingham, Adele Ann (1994). Unbroken Chains. Explorations into the Jaffna Dowry System. Jaffna: Malathi Press.

Balasingham, Adele Ann (1993). Women Fighters of Liberation Tigers. Jaffna, Tamil Eelam: Thasan Printers.

Beck, Brenda E. F. (1982). The three twins. The telling of a South Indian Folk Epic. Bloomington: Indiana University Press.

Bloom, Mia (2005). Dying to Kill The Allure of Suicide Terror. New York: Columbia University Press.

Ca<u>n</u>mukaliṅka<u>n</u>, N. (2002). Paṇpāṭṭi<u>n</u> camūkaviyal. Tellippalai: Nākalingam Nūlālayam.

Chenoy, Anuradha M. (2002). Militarism and Women in South Asia. New Delhi: Kali for Women.

Chenoy, Anuradha M. (2004). Gender and International Politics: The Intersections of Patriarchy and Militarisation. *Indian Journal of Gender Studies* 11, 1: 27-42.

Coomaraswamy, Radhika (2002). Violence, Armed Conflict and the Community. Jayaweera, Swarna, Women in Post-Independence Sri Lanka. New Delhi: Sage: 80-98.

de Cataldo Neuburger, Luisella and Valentini, Tiziana (eds.) (1996). Women and terrorism. New York: St. Martin's Press.

de Mel, Neloufer (2001). Women and the Nation's Narrative. Gender and Nationalism in Twentieth Century Sri Lanka. Colombo: Social Scientists' Association.

de Mel, Neloufer (2004). Body Politics. (Re)Cognising the Female Suicide Bomber in Sri Lanka. *Indian Journal of Gender Studies* 11, 1: 75-93.

Gawankar, Rohini (2003). The Women's Regiment and Capt. Lakshmi of INA. An Untold Episode of NRI Women's Contribution to Indian Freedom Struggle. New Delhi: Devika Publication.

Goonesekere, Savitri (2002). Constitutions, Governance and Laws. Jayaweera, Swarna, Women in Post-Independence Sri Lanka. New Delhi: Sage: 41-78.

Gopinath, Aruna, National Archives of Malaysia. Shivadas, P. C. (eds.) (2007). Footprints on the Sands of Time: Rasammah Bhupalan a Life of Purpose. Kuala Lumpur.

Hellmann-Rajanayagam, Dagmar (1994). The Tigers—Armed Struggle for Identity, Beiträge zur Südasienforschung 157. Stuttgart: Franz Steiner (Reprint 1998).

Hellmann-Rajanayagam, Dagmar (2004). From Differences to Ethnic Solidarity Among the Tamils. Pp. 102-125 in Morrison, Barrie *et al.* (eds.), Struggling to Create a New Society: Sri Lanka in the Era of Globalization. New Delhi: Sage.

Hellmann-Rajanayagam, Dagmar (2008). God My Sister. Fleschenberg, Andrea and Hellmann-Rajanayagam, Dagmar (eds.), Goddesses, Heroes, Martyrs. Berlin: Lit-Verlag, forthcoming.

Hellmann-Rajanayagam, Dagmar (1989). Arumuka Navalar: Religious Reformer or National Leader of Eelam? Indian Economic and Social His-tory Review 26, 2: 235-257.

Hellmann-Rajanayagam, Dagmar (2007). Ausgewählt für Selbstmordkommandos: Die Schwarzen Tiger. Wissenschaft und Frieden 1: 18-21.

Hellmann-Rajanayagam, Dagmar (2008a). The Living Sacrifice. Fleschenberg/Hellmann-Rajanayagam, Goddesses, Heroes, Sacrifices. Berlin: LIT-Verlag (forthcoming).

Hellmann-Rajanayagam, Dagmar (2005). And Heroes Die: Poetry of The Tamil Liberation Movement In Northern Sri Lanka. *South Asia*, New Series, Vol. XXVIII, No. 1 (April): 112-153.

Hellmann-Rajanayagam, Dagmar (2007a). Von Jaffna nach Kilinocchi-Ursprünge und Entwicklung ethnischer Konflikte in Sri Lanka seit dem 19. Jh.- Wechselwirkungen religiös-nationaler Erneuerungsbewegungen und britischer Verwaltungs-und Verfassungspolitik. Ergon: Würzburg.

Iḷaṅkōvaṭikaḷ aruḷicceyta Cilappatikāra mūlamum arumbatavuraiyum aṭiyārkkunallāruraiyum (1978). Madras T.akmt.ar U.Vē. Cāminātaiyar Nūklnilaiyam.

Jayawardene, Kumari (2000). Nobodies to Somebodies. The Rise of the Colonial Bourgeosie in Sri Lanka. Colombo: Social Scientists' Association.

Jayawardena, Kishali Pinto and Kodikara, Chulani (2002). Sri Lanka. Tambiah, Yasmin (ed.), Women and Governance in South Asia. Re-imagining the State. Colombo: ICES.

Mukta, Parita (2004). Gender, Community and Nation: The Myth of Innocence. Pp. 163-178 in Jacobs, Susie M., Jacobson, Ruth Marchbank, Jennifer (eds.), States of Conflict: Gender, Violence and Resistance. London: Zed Books.

Mutukistna, H. F. (1862). The Thesawaleme or the Laws and Customs of Jaffna. Jaffna.

Perera, Morina and Chandrasekera, Rasika (eds.) (2005). Excluding Women. The Struggle for Women's Political Participation in Sri Lanka. Colombo: Social Scientists' Association.

Pfaffenberger, Bryan (1982). Caste in Tamil Culture. The Foundations of Sudra Domination in Tamil Sri Lanka. Bombay.

Puṟanāṉūṟu 276, 277, 278, 279.

Rajasingham-Senanayake, Darini (2001). Ambivalent Empowerment Midst Tragedy of Tamil Women in Conflict. Pp. 104-130 in Manchanda, Rita (ed.), Women in Conflict. New Delhi.

Sarvan, Charles (1998). Appointment with Rajiv Gandhi. Pp. 357-361 in Roberts, Michael (ed.), Sri Lanka: Collective Identities Revisited, Vol. 2. Colombo: Marga.

Schalk, Peter (1994). Women Fighters of the Liberation Tigers in Tamil Ilam. The Martial Feminism of Atel Palacinkam. South Asia Research, Vol. 14, 2 Autumn: 163-183.

Schröter, Susanne (2008). Female leadership in Islamic societies, past and present. Fleschenberg/Hellmann-Rajanayagam, Goddesses, Heroes, Sacrifices. Berlin: LIT-Verlag (forthcoming).

Skaine, Rosemarie (2006). Female Suicide Bombers. London: McFarland.

Thambiah, H. W. (1950). The Laws and Customs of the Tamils of Jaffna. Jaffna.

Trawick, Margaret (1999). Reasons for Violence: A Preliminary Ethnographic Account of the LTTE. In Gamage, Siri and Watson, I.B. (eds.), Conflict and Community in Contemporary Sri Lanka. 'Pearl of the East' or the 'Island of Tears'? New Delhi.

Victor, Barbara (2003). Army of Roses: Inside the World of Palestinian Women Suicide Bombers. New York: Rhodale Press.

Viswanathan-Peterson, Indira (1998). The Tie that Binds: Brothers and Sisters in North and South India. South Asian Social Scientist IV, 1: 25-52.

Ward Fay, Peter (1995). The Forgotten Army: India's Armed Struggle for Independence 1942-1945. Ann Arbor: University of Michigan Press.

Whitworth, Sandra (2006). Men, Militarism & UN Peacekeeping. A Gendered Analysis. New Delhi: Manohar.

Interviews and conversations:

Anonymous, November 2007.

Coomaraswamy, Radhika, Former Spezial UN-envoy for Violence Against Women and Children, August 2005.

Kalaivilly, Yo., Chairwoman Women's Wing Jaffna, 25th February 2004. SLMM officer, March 2003.

Thamilini, Su, Leader, Women's Political Wing LTTE, 2nd March 2004, 5th March 2004 and 30th August 2007.

Internet Sources

Balasingham, Adele Ann, Women Fighters of Liberation Tigers. *http:/ /www.tamilnation.org/ books/Eelam/ adeleann.htm* accessed on 6th January 2008.

Bomb targets Sri Lanka army chief. *http://news.bbc.co.uk/2/hi/ south_asia/4941744.stm* accessed 3rd January 2008.

Colombo to annul CFA, *http://www.tamilnet.com/art.html?catid= 13&artid=24157* (a), accessed 3rd January 2008.

Eelam Map, *http://www.geocities.com/capitolHill/senate/4745/ map.html* accessed 7th January 2008.

Government Minister Escapes Suicide Attack in Sri Lanka, International Herald Tribune. *http:// www.iht.com/articles/ 2007/11/28/europe/lanka.php?WT.mc_id= rssasia* accessed 3rd January 2008.

http://www.tamilnation.org/hundredtamils/annai_poopathy.htm accessed on 1st January 2008.

http://www.tamilnet.com/art.html?catid=13&artid=13106 accessed on 1st January 2008.

Sathyam Art Gallery Tamil Eelam Freedom Struggle–Paintings *http:/ /www. tamilnation.org/art/struggle/ rajah.htm* accessed 6th January 2008.

Sathyam Art Gallery Tamil Eelam Freedom Struggle–Paintings. *http:// www.Ta-mil-nation.org/art/struggle/ neethan/index.htm* accessed 6th January 2008.

Sathyam Art Gallery Tamil Eelam Freedom Struggle–Paintings. *http:/ /www.Tamil nation.org/art/ struggle/malathi.htm* accessed 6th January 2008

Selbstmordattentäterin trägt Sprengstoff im BH. *http://www.spiegel.de/ politik/ausland/0,15 18,520159,00.html* accessed 3rd January 2008.

Thileepan, an Epitome of Sacrifice and Symbolism of Determination *http://www.ltteps.org/? view= 320&folder=2* accessed 3rd January 2008.

Trawick Margaret, 'War and Tamil Women: A Women's Eye-view 1990, *http://www. tamilnation.org/forum/trawick/90000.htm* accessed 6th January 2008.

3

CONTESTATIONS REGARDING IDENTITY, NATIONALISM AND CITIZENSHIP DURING THE STRUGGLES OF THE INDIGENOUS PEOPLES OF THE CHITTAGONG HILL TRACTS OF BANGLADESH

SHAPAN ADNAN

In the hilly and forested fringes of southeastern Bangladesh, the indigenous peoples of the Chittagong Hill Tracts (CHT) have been struggling with threats to their material and cultural conditions integral to retaining their own ethnic identity.[2] Indeed, such threats faced by ethnic minorities in the region have been aggravated by the impacts of the in-migration by settlers, land alienation, and counterproductive development interventions. As discussed below, the experience of the indigenous peoples of the CHT graphically illustrates the ways in which such factors have threatened the identity and citizenship rights of small sub-national groups, generating ethnic nationalism as a means of defense as well as a platform for demanding fully-fledged citizenship rights and due protection from the state.

Social and Historical Background

The Chittagong Hill Tracts (CHT) of Bangladesh lies on the country's international borders with Myanmar (Burma) and

India (the 'states' of Tripura and Mizoram), as shown in the map. The present boundaries of the CHT were carved out of the British colonial empire in 1860 [Roy, 1995: 53; Mohsin, 1997: 26] and demarcated as a new district of the province of Bengal (by Act No. XXII). The region was sub-divided into the three smaller districts of Rangamati, Bandarban and Khagrachhari during the last quarter of the twentieth century.

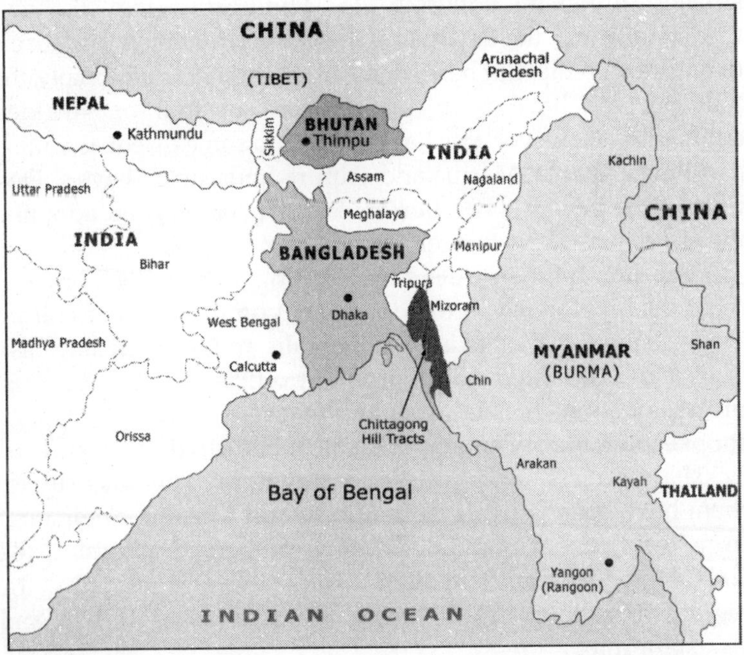

The Chittagong Hill Tracts of Bangladesh in Regional Perspective

The CHT has been historically inhabited by 'tribal' groups or indigenous peoples, with a sprinkling of non-tribals from the plains. The former consists of around a dozen tribes or ethnic groups, the largest of which are the Chakma, the Marma and the Tripura, in that order. Among the smaller groups are the Mru, the Tanchainghya, the Bawm (or Bom), the Khumi, the Khyang, the Lushai (or Mizo), the Pankho, and the Chak (or Sak) [Sopher, 1964; Brauns & Loffler, 1990: 34; Roy, 1994: 11;

1998b: 3; Adnan, 2004: 10-13]. These ethnic minorities, taken together, are locally known as the Pahari or Hill peoples of the CHT (also termed Hillmen in colonial parlance). They differ markedly from the non-hillmen of the plains in terms of physical appearance, language, religion and cultural practices, while having much greater resemblance with the tribal groups of northeastern India and Myanmar. Most of the Hill peoples of the CHT are Buddhist (e.g. the Chakma and the Marma), with much smaller numbers adhering to Hinduism (the Tripura), Christianity (e.g. the Bawm and the Lushai), animism and forms of nature worship, but hardly any are Muslims. Traditionally, the Hill peoples have been practitioners of *jum* or swidden cultivation. However, this has changed to some extent as valley-dwelling Chakma, Marma and Tripura households have shifted from *jum* to plough cultivation of wet rice over the years, adopting the techniques of the Bengali peasantry of the plains.

The non-hillmen outsiders residing in the CHT have in most cases belonged to the dominant community and culture at the centre (i.e. the Pakistanis, Bengalis and/or Bangladeshis). They have consisted of government officials, security forces, professionals such as lawyers and teachers, as well as traders, shopkeepers, moneylenders, craftsmen, industrial wage workers, rickshaw-pullers, and peasant cultivators. The majority of them have been Bengali, both Hindu and Muslim, originating from the densely populated plains of Bengal adjoining the CHT. However, non-Bengali outsiders have also resided in the region at various times during the periods of British and Pakistani rule.

Changes in Administrative and Political Status

The CHT Regulation, enacted in 1900 by the British colonial state, has provided the basic legal framework of civil, revenue and judicial administration of the CHT during the subsequent period.[3] Its original provisions on the rights of entry and residence, as well as rules of land settlement and transfer in the CHT, were intended to give special protection to the rights of the Hill peoples, while also attempting to check entry and land settlement by non-hillmen from outside. Subsequently, the

British became concerned to isolate the region and its Hill peoples from the rest of Bengal administratively and politically [van Schendel, 1995: 134]. In 1920, the CHT was declared a 'Backward Tract', which was to be administered as an 'Excluded Area' [Mohsin, 1997: 34; Roy, 1997b: 11; R.C.K. Roy, 1996: 19]. The Government of India Act of 1935 designated the region as a 'Totally Excluded Area'.

During the Partition of British India in 1947, the CHT was annexed to the Muslim-majority state of Pakistan, despite the unwillingness of the leaders of the Hill peoples [Mohsin, 1997: 35-37]. The constitution of Pakistan, promulgated in 1956, retained the status of the CHT as an 'Excluded Area' [Shelley, 1992: 30]. However, the Pakistani government was interested in exploiting the rich natural resources of the CHT, and showed little concern about the possible adverse impacts on the Hill peoples and their habitat [Mohsin, 1997: 45]. In this new post-colonial dispensation, the erstwhile colonial policy of keeping the CHT isolated from the rest of the country became an impediment for Bengali interest groups concerned to lift the restrictions on their entry, residence and rights to hold landed property in the area [van Schendel, 1995: 136]. As a result, the status of the CHT was altered from an 'Excluded Area' to a 'Tribal Area' in the new constitution adopted by Pakistan in 1962. The limited protection provided by even this modified status was stripped away by a constitutional amendment in 1964 and other administrative and judicial interventions [Mohsin, 1997: 105; Adnan, 2004: 22-23].

Adverse Impacts of the Kaptai Hydro-Electricity Project

In parallel, certain development interventions had critical impacts on the CHT, profoundly altering its socio-economic conditions and demographic structure. Foremost among these was the Kaptai hydroelectricity project built during the early 1960s [Adnan, 2004: 23-24]. Its artificial reservoir submerged huge swathes of land containing human settlements and arable areas. The aggregate stock of cultivable and forested lands in the CHT was substantially reduced, as a result of which swidden cultivation in the remaining areas was dangerously intensified, leading to excessive exploitation and degradation of the soil [CHTDP, 1987: 2; Brauns & Loffler, 1990: 40; Roy, 1995: 65-66; Mohsin, 1997: 104; Adnan, 2004: 44-46]. Of the total Pahari population of 335,000 in the CHT[4], approximately 80,000-100,000 were forced to move from their farms and homesteads, without adequate compensation or rehabilitation [Sopher, 1963: 347-360; Roy, 1996a: 5; [R.C.K. Roy, 1996: 64]. Mohsin, 1997: 102-103; Adnan, 2004: 23-24, 44-46]. Around 30,000 displaced Chakmas crossed over the Indian border, becoming international refugees who were subsequently settled in the states of Tripura, Mizoram and Arunachal Pradesh in northeastern India. Another 20,000 Hill peoples are reported to have moved as international refugees to Myanmar [Hazarika, 1994: 282]. Thousands of other uprooted Hill peoples became internally displaced persons (IDP) scattered in the rural interior of the CHT, mostly encroaching into the remote Reserve Forest areas to eke out a subsistence [Hume, 1999].

New opportunities for employment and business in the CHT created by the Kaptai project and other development programmes were mostly taken up by non-hillmen, who included both Bengali and non-Bengali citizens of Pakistan [Mohsin, 1997: 46, 105]. Government jobs in the CHT were largely given to non-Pahari employees from outside. Virtually all wholesale and retail trade, transport services, financial businesses and moneylending activities in the region were controlled by outsiders, the bulk of whom were Bengalis. Despite the existence of legal restrictions to the entry of outsiders, administrative policies of the local state tacitly facilitated their in-migration during the post-Kaptai years [Ali, 1993: 177]. The proportion of Bengalis in the total CHT population rose from 13% to 19% between 1961 and 1974, while that of the Hill peoples declined correspondingly [Adnan, 2004: 55-57, Table 1].

Impacts of the Bengali-Pakistani Conflict and Indo-Pak war of 1971

During the 1960s, economic disparity and political stresses within the federal polity of Pakistan led to the growth of a

Bengali nationalist movement in its eastern wing, spearheaded by Sheikh Mujibur Rahman, the charismatic leader of the Awami League [Mohsin 1997: 50-56]. The ensuing conflict resulted in a brutal crackdown by the Pakistani army on the Bengali populace of East Pakistan on 26 March 1971. In response, Bengali nationalist guerrillas, known as the Mukti Bahini (Freedom Fighters) began an armed resistance against the Pakistani occupying forces, which subsequently became known as the liberation struggle of Bangladesh. The Indian security forces gave clandestine support to the Mukti Bahini and subsequently became directly involved in open war with Pakistan, which ended with the surrender of the Pakistani forces in Dhaka on 16 December 1971.

This complex chain of events led to not only the break up of the federal polity of Pakistan but also the transformation of the former province of East Pakistan into the independent state of Bangladesh. Significantly, constructs of neither the Pakistani nor the Bangladeshi nation had any space for accommodating the Hill peoples of the CHT, who were definitionally excluded from both of these 'imagined communities' [Mohsin, 1997: 43-45]. Not surprisingly, most Paharis remained indifferent to the Pakistani-Bengali conflict during 1971. However, some were caught up inexorably in the ensuing crossfire. Due to limited collaboration with the Pakistani regime by a very small minority of the Hill peoples, there arose a widespread misconception that the Paharis as a whole had opposed the struggle for Bangladesh. Tragically, this provided the pretext for drastic acts of 'revenge' against the Hill peoples by some Bengali groups, including misguided elements of the Mukti Bahini, during the last phase of the 1971 war and its immediate aftermath [Shelley, 1992: 33 and 109; Ali, 1993: 183-184; Mohsin, 1997: 58 and 165; Adnan, 2004: 25].

Alienation of the Paharis in independent Bangladesh

Early in 1972, leaders of the Hill peoples decided to approach the new government of Bangladesh to seek protection from further assault on their lives and property by vengeful Bengalis and obtain constitutional recognition of their rights as ethnic minority groups. Disturbingly, however, the Pahari delegations failed to get any assurances from the government regarding protection from such acts of misconstrued 'revenge', as well as their demand to be recognized as groups with distinct cultural identities. On the contrary, Prime Minister Sheikh Mujibur Rahman is reported to have advised them to 'become Bengali' and assimilate themselves into this hegemonic identity [Hazarika, 1994: 278; Mohsin, 1997: 58]. Paradoxically, the demand of the Hill peoples for protection of their lands, lives and cultural identities was perceived by the government as *secessionist* and deemed to be a threat to national security. The Paharis were treated as a 'rebel' community and punitive military raids against their settlements in the CHT were carried out almost immediately afterwards by the Bangladeshi security forces [Mey, 1984: 114; Mohsin, 1997: 58].

In response, a political party was set up on 7 March 1972 to represent the interests of the Hill peoples under the leadership of Manabendra Narayan Larma, named *Parbatya Chattagram Jana Samhati Samiti* (PCJSS) [Ali, 1993: 184; Mohsin, 1997: 57-58 and 165].[5] The PCJSS propagated 'Jumma' nationalism and a collective 'Jumma' identity, based on the idea that all the various Pahari groups shared the tradition of *jum* (swidden) cultivation in common. Another crucial step was the formation of a military wing of the PCJSS in early 1973, known as the Shanti Bahini (SB), in order to resist the Bangladeshi state and its security forces [Shelley, 1992: 111].

In November 1972, the Bangladesh parliament adopted a new constitution that unilaterally imposed a common 'Bengali' identity on all groups inhabiting the country, regardless of their linguistic and ethnic diversity. Far from providing guarantees protecting the distinct culture, identity and life-styles of the Hill peoples within the framework of a plural socicty, it served to institutionalize hegemonic Bengali nationalism and a policy of forced assimilation towards culturally distinct minority groups [Mohsin, 1997: 59, fn.].

During 1972-75, a state of low-intensity warfare prevailed in the CHT for a number of considerations related to domestic security and foreign insurgency [Mohsin, 1997: 166, fn; Brauns &

Loffler, 1990: 241]. In particular, the Bengali-dominated government and military establishment suspected that the Hill peoples were being mobilized for a secessionist movement, purportedly posing a threat to national security. As a result of such considerations, the armed forces became involved in raiding the settlements of the Hill peoples and perpetrating violent atrocities [Mohsin, 1997: 166].

The situation took a critical turn after 15 August 1975, when Prime Minister Mujib was assassinated and the Awami League government ousted from power by an army coup d'etat. Following a few months of turbulence, General (and, subsequently, President) Ziaur Rahman emerged as the military strongman of the country. Even though the PCJSS was the principal political platform of the Hill peoples, the Zia regime banned the organization, forcing the leaders of the party to seek refuge in India [Mohsin, 1997: 66-67; Shelley, 1992: 111]. This constituted the turning point when the Pahari leadership lost all hope of reaching political accommodation within the constitutional framework of Bangladesh, triggering a move towards armed insurgency.

Significantly, relations between the governments of India and Bangladesh had also become strained at this stage.[6] The Indian government decided to allow the PCJSS and the Shanti Bahini to set up bases in the states of Tripura and Mizoram adjoining the CHT. Furthermore, Indian agencies provided the Shanti Bahini with covert military training and arms supplies, enabling its guerrilla units to undertake operations inside the CHT against the Bangladeshi security forces [Hazarika, 1994: 279-280; Bhaumik, 1996; Brauns & Loffler, 1990: 242; Shelley, 1992: 126-129; Ali, 1993: 187-191; Mohsin, 1997: 167-168].

Counter-Insurgency and Demographic Engineering

The regime under General Zia responded to these Shanti Bahini attacks by launching full-scale counter-insurgency operations from late 1976. It displayed little understanding of the root causes that had driven the Hill peoples into armed rebellion, blaming it simply on the 'lack of economic development' among them and the fact that the CHT was "a backward area without basic infrastructure for development and an organized market system, and had a primitive mode of cultivation" [Shelley, 1992: 129]. In this official view of things, the deeper anxieties and apprehensions of the Hill peoples, confronted by growing threats to their cultural identity, habitat, and culture were conveniently overlooked.

In addition to military brutality, the counter-insurgency strategy of the Zia regime incorporated *demographic engineering* as a means of increasing the number of Bengalis in the CHT at the expense of the Hill peoples. This consisted of a two-pronged operation, the first of which involved use of violence and arson to evict Paharis from their lands and villages and 'regroup' them into camps and 'cluster villages' under military surveillance [R.C.K. Roy, 1996: 79; Hume, 1999: 4; Ali, 1993: 190-193; Roy, 1997c: 183]. Approximately, 100,000 Hill peoples were forcibly evicted from their homes and lands, around 55,000 of whom are estimated to have fled across the international border to the Indian states of Tripura and Mizoram, eking out a miserable existence in refugee camps [Ali, 1993: 193; R.C.K. Roy, 1996: 78; Roy, 1997c: 168]. Another 30,000-50,000 were forced by military and settler attacks to seek shelter in the mountainous tracts and forests in the interior of the CHT, becoming internally displaced persons (IDP) [Roy, 1998b: 7; Hume, 1999].

The second component of demographic engineering involved bringing in massive numbers of landless Bengali settlers from the plains through state-managed transmigration. These settlers were also promised homestead and arable lands in the CHT, and government officials forcibly (and illegally) allotted the lands of the Hill peoples to them for this purpose [R.C.K. Roy, 1996: 78 and 94-96; Hume, 1999: 4]. These planned population transfers, begun in 1978-79 and continued up to 1984-85, led to the *net* addition of 300,000-340,000 settlers to the CHT population, virtually all of whom were landless Bengali Muslim peasants [Adnan, 2004: 47-53]. The political objective of these transmigration and land redistribution operations was to accelerate the settlement of a sizeable Bengali population in the CHT that could be counted upon to be loyal to the

Bangladeshi state. The success of demographic engineering as a means of counter-insurgency was evident in the accelerated growth of Bengalis from 19% of the total population of the CHT in 1974 to 49% in 1991, while the Pahari population fell drastically from 81% to 51% over the same 17-year period.[7]

The dynamics of the ethnic conflict in the CHT did not remain confined to purely military targets consisting of the 'armed' forces on both sides (i.e. the Bangladeshi security forces and the Shanti Bahini). On the contrary, armed attacks inexorably spread to the respective *non-combatant* civilian populations, irrespective of whether they had been responsible for any violence [Roy, 1997c: 168; 1996b]. Gross human rights violations were perpetrated by both sides in this bitter ethnic conflict, but there is little doubt that the Hill peoples were the victims of much greater human rights violations perpetrated upon them by the security forces and sections of the Bengali settlers [Shelley, 1992: 123-125; Ali, 1993: 165; Loffler, 1991: 28; Mohsin, 1997: 185]. Between 1980 and the 1990s, at least 11 major massacres of the Hill peoples by Bengali forces were reported [Mohsin, 1998: 116; Roy, 1997c: 183]. Furthermore, the security forces were also responsible for widespread raping of Pahari women, which was systematically used as an instrument of humiliating and devaluing the ethnic identity and nationalism of the Hill peoples [Mohsin, 1997: 178; 1998: 116].

These counter-insurgency measures predictably provoked retaliation by the guerrilla forces of the Shanti Bahini and gave justification to their counter-violence. Settlements of the Bengali migrants became prime objects of their attack, constituting 'soft targets', compared to the 'hard' military ones [Brauns & Loffler, 1990: 242; Ali, 1993: 190-193]. The aim of the violent attacks of the Shanti Bahini was to force the Bengali settlers to leave the CHT and thereby also regain the lands of the Hill peoples that they had taken over.

Shift in Counter-Insurgency Strategy Towards Co-option

While the counter-insurgency operations by the security forces failed to crush the resistance of the Hill peoples, the mounting costs of maintaining a large body of troops in the CHT became prohibitively expensive. These considerations led to a significant shift towards a 'softer' strategy of *co-opting* the Hill peoples into networks of patronage and privilege. This policy change was initiated by General Ershad, who captured power in 1982, following the assassination of President Zia in 1981. In October 1983, the Ershad regime declared its willingness to suspend further transmigration of Bengali settlers to the CHT and initiate direct dialogue with the PCJSS, while granting amnesty to Pahari rebels [Shelley, 1992: 139]. In 1985, the regime announced a set of new policies and programmes for the economic development of the CHT, with the aim of integrating 'tribals and non-tribals'. This indicated that the policy of assimilating the Hill peoples into the dominant national culture was still at work, despite the shift in strategy. The regime also allocated large amounts of resources to the so-called programmes of 'pacification' of the Hill peoples, concerned with "confidence-building measure geared to winning hearts and minds of people", undertaken by the security forces in collaboration with the civil administration [Shelley, 1992: 157].

During the second half of the 1980s, the Ershad regime proffered a wide range of incentives and concessions to win over the Hill peoples. Among these were reservation of seats in institutions of higher education, jobs in government departments and scheduled banks, as well as contracts for development projects and public works [Shelley, 1992: 136-139]. It placated Pahari demands for local self-government by establishing Hill District Local Government Councils (HDLGC) in the CHT in 1989 [Brauns & Loffler, 1990: 244; Shelley,1992: 142-143; Ali, 1993: 194; Mohsin, 1997: 74, 202-203].

Furthermore, the regime offered various inducements to encourage existing cadres of the PCJSS/SB to give up the struggle and return to normal life, making use of public funds and development resources to co-opt the Hill peoples into the lucrative networks of state patronage. In fact, these offers of amnesty and patronage succeeded in encouraging significant numbers to defect from the ranks of the PCJSS/SB during the 1980s [Shelley, 1992: 147]. Indeed, these softer forms of counter-insurgency succeeded in weakening the social support-base of Pahari resistance to an extent that had not been possible earlier with the blunter instruments of brute violence and forced displacement.

The Peace Accord and its aftermath

In December 1990, General Ershad was toppled from power by popular protests across the country, leading to the restoration of parliamentary democracy. Elections held in 1991 brought to power the Bangladesh Nationalist Party (BNP), headed by Prime Minister Khaleda Zia. Despite a sustained ceasefire and several rounds of negotiations with the PCJSS, however, no formal agreement was reached by this BNP government during its tenure (1991-96) [Shelley, 1992: 148, 170-171; Mohsin, 1997: 74].

However, the 1996 parliamentary elections resulted in an Awami League government under the leadership of Prime Minister Sheikh Hasina. Relations between the governments of India and Bangladesh improved, given the former's favourable disposition towards the Awami League. Discernible combat fatigue among the Hill peoples was reinforced by pressure from the Indian government on the PCJSS/SB as well as the government of Bangladesh to reach a political settlement [Mohsin, 1997: 177, fn. 17; 1998: 115]. After several rounds of negotiations, a Peace Accord was eventually signed between accredited representatives of the Government of Bangladesh and the PCJSS on 2 December 1997.[8]

The Accord led to the surrender of the members of the PCJSS/SB along with the de-commissioning of their arms. The government provided general amnesty and rehabilitation facilities to the PCJSS/SB members returning to normal life. It also agreed to the repatriation of Pahari refugees from India and rehabilitation of the internally displaced Paharis scattered around the CHT. Several wide-ranging measures for resolving land-related disputes and problems were accepted by the government. The Peace Accord also redefined the status and powers of the existing district councils of the CHT, re-naming these as Hill District Councils (HDC). Furthermore, a new body called the Regional Council (RC) was established with jurisdiction over the entire CHT, overarching its three districts. However, the extent of devolution of power was quite limited, and the decisions made by these councils clearly remained subject to the concurrence of the national government, which retained control over their purse strings and had the final say on all substantive matters. Crucially, the Peace Accord was not backed by any constitutional guarantee or legal act, making it susceptible to potential violation and modification by subsequent governments [Roy, 1998].

A section of the Bengali population and settler organizations vehemently rejected the Peace Accord. So did major national-level political forces including the Bangladesh Nationalist Party (BNP) and the fundamentalist Jamaat-e-Islami, as well as smaller right-wing and pro-Islamic political parties and organizations. In their view, the Accord had made 'too many concessions to Pahari interests', while converting Bengalis in the CHT into 'second class citizens' who were denied their due constitutional rights [Mohsin, 1998: 107].

The decade following the Peace Accord provided a test period for assessing the good faith of the two parties in implementing its provisions. The PCJSS/SB leaders and cadres rejoined civil life and took up the positions in local self-government that were made available after the truce. However, the Awami League government (1996-2001), having signed the Accord, failed to implement many of its substantive clauses – allegedly, for fear of losing support (and votes) among the dominant Bengali community. Significantly, the Bangladesh Nationalist Party (BNP) and the Jamaat-e-Islami, which had publicly rejected the Accord when in opposition, were not even interested in implementing the clauses of the treaty when they became the major partners of the subsequent elected government (2001-06). Indeed, many violations of the Accord took place under this government, which resulted in partially reversing the peace process and reactivating the very factors that had precipitated the ethnic conflict in the first place. In particular, the continuation of settler in-migration, forced land acquisition, as well as human rights violation in the form of killings and rape have generated widespread disillusionment among the Hill peoples, such that they no longer believe that the government has the will to implement the Peace Accord.

The key events marking the struggle of the Hill peoples against the state and the dominant Bengali community have been briefly outlined above. These provide the factual basis for analyzing the various contestations pertaining to identity, nationalism and citizenship thrown up by the struggle, as taken up below.

Ethnicity and Innovation in Identity Formation

The British recognized the Hill peoples as a special category among their colonial subjects, whose distinctive ethnic identities, cultural traits and natural habitat in the forested uplands of the CHT needed to be protected from encroachment of outsiders. This concern is embodied in the CHT Regulation of 1900 in terms of restrictions on the entry, residence and property-holding rights of non-hillmen. While some of these protective clauses were relaxed during the last decades of British rule, the Hill peoples continued to be protected, as well as isolated, by the special status given to their identity and habitat by the colonial state. However, these measures began to be undermined under the post-colonial order in Pakistan, because they constrained the exploitation of the CHT resources by the state and the market. None the less, there was still some recognition of tribal identity and status, while non-hillmen outsiders were legally restricted from holding land rights in the region almost until the end of Pakistan rule.

However, in the new state of Bangladesh, there was virtually no legal-constitutional recognition or protection of the Hill people's identities, cultures and minority rights. This was somewhat paradoxical, since Bangladesh itself had emerged through a struggle for recognition of the Bengali identity, language and culture against the Pakistani military regime. Indeed, there was little sympathy in the Bangladeshi government for the Hill peoples' plea for recognition and protection, which was viewed as being 'secessionist' and 'subversive'. The identities of the Hill peoples thus became subject to the combined pressures of (a) the assimilationist project of the Bangladeshi nation-state and (b) encroachment into their natural habitat by Bengali migrants, state-sponsored settlers and the security forces.

Consequently, the crystallization of the collective Jumma identity of the Hill peoples can be viewed as being driven by the need to distance themselves from this Bengali assimilationist project. It was essentially identity formulation by *negation*–in contradistinction to the identity of the dominant Bengali population. Articulated by the PCJSS and the Shanti Bahini, the Jumma identity was deployed in the armed resistance of the Hill peoples against the Bengali-dominated state. Ironically, even though the struggle led to their distinctive identities being recognized by some clauses of the Peace Accord, this was still in terms of non-specified 'tribal groups' rather than as ethnic peoples with specific names and features.

The identities of the Hill peoples have also been influenced by ongoing processes of demographic change and globalization, as modified by the impact of the armed conflict. Rural out-migration to urban areas has been accelerated by the violence and insecurity affecting Pahari society during several decades of counter-insurgency. In addition to many Paharis who have become residents of urban areas of Bangladesh, a small proportion has migrated to India as well as various countries of Europe, North America and Australasia. For such migrants, there has been some erosion of Pahari identities through adoption of urban and global life-styles. At the same time, diaspora-based Pahari activist groups have consciously attempted to re-assert their identity and grievances in the international arena.

Contestation between Rival Nationalism

During most of the twentieth century, the Hill peoples were essentially passive spectators to contestations between rival nationalisms espoused by dominant groups. Initially they were incorporated against their will into the state of Pakistan, which was created by Muslim nationalism concerned to create a separate polity in which Muslims would form the majority, and thereby become free of Hindu domination. Subsequently, conflict within the Muslim polity of Pakistan gave rise of Bengali nationalism in East Pakistan, which began to contest the hegemony of Muslim nationalism. It was aimed at resisting political domination of West Pakistani elite groups, resolving economic disparity between the eastern and western wings of the country, and ending discrimination against Bengalis, who were treated as second class citizens by the Pakistani administration. However, the Pakistani regime viewed the growth of Bengali nationalism as secessionist, and launched a military crackdown on the Bengali population in East Pakistan to pre-empt any such outcome.

Even though Bengali nationalism did not explicitly include the Hill peoples, it is significant that one of the Pahari chiefs, several senior leaders and some young men did try to support the cause of Bengali nationalism against Pakistani repression [Adnan, 2004: 25]. Some of them crossed over to India but found themselves distrusted and cold-shouldered by Awami League party bosses and Indian intelligence officials [Shelley, 1992: 33; Ali, 1993: 182-183]. Attempts by some of the Hill peoples to express solidarity with the cause of Bengali nationalism during 1971 were thus rebuffed at the very outset.

As noted earlier, the new constitution of Bangladesh explicitly incorporated a hegemonic form of Bengali nationalism that simply suffocated all other linguistic or ethnic identities and nationalisms among the people of the country. However, this kind of chauvinistic intolerance backfired and made the Bangladeshi nation-state *weaker,* rather than stronger, by alienating the Hill peoples and precipitating an ethnic conflict that sapped the strength and resources of the country. The situation did not improve when the Zia regime supplanted Bengali nationalism with Bangladeshi nationalism. While the latter did nominally provide room for non-Bengali elements in the construct of the nation, in practice it treated them as subordinate to Bengalis.

In sum, these various nationalisms–Muslim and Pakistani, Bengali and Bangladeshi–were espoused by the dominant groups controlling state power in the Pakistani and Bangladeshi nation-states respectively. These hegemonic ideologies served to subordinate groups such as the Paharis of the CHT, excluding or marginalizing them from the national mainstream.

Emergence of nationalism among the Hill peoples thus took place in *reaction* to the assimilationist ideologies of the nation-state propagated by the regimes in power, viz. Pakistani, Bengali, or Bangladeshi nationalism. The process was aided by the expansion of education and literacy among Paharis, particularly the Chakma community, and the rise in social and political consciousness among them following the devastating impacts of the Kaptai project and the growing in-migration of non-hillmen. Like the Jumma identity, the Jumma nationalism embracing all Pahari ethnic groups was deliberately constructed and propagated by the PCJSS and SB in order to unify them in the political and military struggle against the hegemony of Bengali/Bangladeshi nationalism. Thus, the emergence of Jumma ethnic nationalism among the Hill peoples was also based on a *negation* of the dominant nationalisms being imposed by groups controlling state power.

It is therefore somewhat ironic that the Peace Accord makes no mention of Jumma nationalism, even though it uses the apellation 'tribal' to describe the Hill peoples. However, the Pahari diasporas in India and the West continue to propagate Jumma nationalism through their networks and publications.

Citizens and Rebels

Despite being created by the politics of Muslim nationalism, Pakistan was not a theocratic state, so that resident non-Muslims, including the Hill peoples, were entitled to be citizens of the country. However, despite this formal status, the Paharis were treated as *de facto* second-class citizens by the government and agencies of the state. This became evident during the rehabilitation of people uprooted by the Kaptai project, when Pahari oustees were given second preference to Bengalis in the allottment of alternative lands for rehabilitation [Sopher, 1963: 348-357]. Many were also harassed and cheated when attempting to get the monetary compensation package to which they were entitled [R.C.K. Roy, 1996: 61]. Among the many thousands of Paharis who were forced to become international refugees, many ended up being stateless, without any citizenship rights in either Pakistan (later Bangladesh) or India, e.g. Chakma refugees who were eventually re-settled in remote Arunachal Pradesh of India [Brauns & Loffler, 1990: 40; Roy, 1996a: 5]. Thousands of other internally displaced Paharis uprooted by the Kaptai project and the subsequent counter-insurgency operations had to live as illegal dwellers in reserve forests, detached from the agencies of the Pakistani (later Bangladeshi) state, effectively lacking any citizenship rights.

During 1971, even though some Paharis attempted to join the Bengali cause against Pakistani occupying forces, they were prevented from doing so by concerned political and military gatekeepers. Subsequently the Hill peoples were misconstrued as being disloyal to the new state of Bangladesh. Their formal status as citizens of the country did not save them from attacks by Bengali vigilante groups seeking 'revenge'. Moreover, the political leadership of the country was unwilling to provide them with any protection against such violence, while juridical and administrative agencies failed to render justice against wrongs done to them by Bengali civilians and the security forces. Despite Pahari pleas to the contrary, the newly crafted constitution of Bangladesh failed to incorporate any provisions recognizing and safeguarding the status and culture of the Hill peoples as citizens belonging to ethnic minorities. Even their attempts to plead their case with the political leadership of the country were misconstrued as harbouring a secessionist agenda. As a result, they were treated as a virtually rebel population and subjected to armed repression by the security forces. These acts marked the beginning of a trajectory in which the Hill peoples were suspected of conspiring against the nation-state which, in turn, triggered off Pahari responses that constituted preparatory steps towards insurgency, e.g. the formation of their own political party (PCJSS) and a military wing (the Shanti Bahini).

Given the absence of any meaningful citizenship status and relationship with the state, the next step in the process was for the Hill peoples to transform themselves from *suspected* to *actual* insurgents, challenging and contesting the authority of the Bengali-dominated state. Indeed, the PCJSS and the Shanti Bahini set up a parallel government in the areas under their control, displacing the Bengali administration and imposing governance through their own forces and cadres, inclusive of collecting taxes and resolving disputes [Adnan, 2004: 28, Box 2.1]. From the vantage-point of the Bangladeshi government and military establishment, the Pahari forces were viewed as committing treason, particularly because the PCJSS/SB were being supported by the Indian state and security forces (even if for opportunistic considerations of national interest on the part the latter). Such transformation of the alienated Paharis from citizens to rebels also embodied the very *negation* of the *duties* of citizenship. It was the inexorable consequence of the denial of the citizenship *rights* of the Hill peoples by the Bangladeshi state, breaking the contract of citizenship.

This metamorphosis in the citizenship status of the Hill peoples was undoubtedly a crucial consideration underlying the demographic engineering strategy undertaken by Bangladesh during the period of counter-insurgency. In effect, the state organized transmigration on a massive scale to expand the Bengali settler population of the CHT, in order to provide a demographic and political counterweight to the support-base of the PCJSS/SB among the Hill peoples [Mohsin, 1998: 113 and 174; Adnan, 2004: 48-52]. The relative weightage of 'loyal citizens' was increased by bringing in Bengali settlers, while simultaneously reducing the numbers of the 'rebellious' Paharis through military operations, massacres, and expulsion as international refugees.

Subsequently, when the Bangladeshi state realized that violent brutalization was not succeeding in crushing the insurgency, it switched to the softer strategy of cooption, attempting to 'pacify' the alienated Pahari community in order to get them to return to being loyal citizens rather than rebels. In continuation of this modified counter-insurgency strategy, the Peace Accord incorporated offers of patronage aimed at giving the Hill peoples a stake in the existing social order. Significantly, however, the Accord was negotiated and signed *within* the framework of the state of Bangladesh, thereby ensuring that the Pahari rebels were brought back to the fold without compromising on national sovereignty.

However, this return to citizenship did not necessarily mean that the position of the Hill peoples improved in all cases. The failure of the Bangladeshi government to implement many of the crucial clauses of the Peace Accord seriously undermined that prospect. Furthermore, many of the disruptive factors that had led to the Pahari insurgency in the first place, such as in-migration and land alienation, continued to operate during the post-Accord decade. Indeed, the position of the Hill peoples has not improved beyond that of being second class citizens, subject to discrimination by the administration and repression by the security forces and Bengali settlers.

Concluding Remarks

The preceding analysis has traced the contestations pertaining to the identity, nationalism, and citizenship of the Hill peoples during their struggle against domination by outsiders backed by the state and its security forces. While their intrinsic identities are based on ethnicity, the forging of a new Jumma-based identity and nationalism shared by all groups was propelled by the concern to counter the assimilationist project of the Bangladeshi nation-state and the destruction of their natural habitat by Bengali settlers and security forces.

Despite their formal status as citizens, the Hill peoples were marginalized and subordinated by the Bangladeshi government not only through legal-constitutional means but also by the direct exercise of state power and violence, including ethnic cleansing and violation of human rights. This was most clearly apparent in the demographic component of the counter-insurgency strategy which aimed at reducing the 'rebel' Pahari population and drastically increasing the proportion of loyal Bengali citizens in the CHT.

Given this context, the counter-attacks by the PCJSS and Shanti Bahini can be seen as attempts to force back settlers and reclaim their alienated lands. Success in such efforts would have provided them with the space where their new-found

Jumma identity and nationalism could have flourished and enabled them to enjoy a kind of *de facto* citizenship based on their own power and institutions.

Despite government and military suspicions to the contrary, the Hill peoples of the CHT were not secessionists bent upon establishing a state for themselves. Rather, they were driven into rebellion by the inconsiderate attitudes and provocative policies of the Bangladeshi government and security forces. In fact, the prime demands of the Hill peoples were that their lives and land rights should be protected by the state and that their distinct cultural identities should be given due recognition in the constitution and laws of the country. None of these expectations was unreasonable, and the government could have easily accommodated them through legal and constitutional amendments and suitable administrative measures, without any substantive loss or limitation of national sovereignty. It follows that the insurgency and ethnic conflict in the CHT could well have been avoided if the government had been far-sighted enough to have ensured that their position and rights as citizens belonging to minority groups were adequately enshrined in the constitution and laws of the country.

Notes

1. This paper draws upon my earlier research and publications, particularly Adnan [2004; 2006].
2. For present purposes, ethnic identity is defined as an indivisible and irreducible social and cultural construct, based on the specific combination of the distinctive physical features, language, culture, life-styles, religious or ritual beliefs characterizing a particular social group. The boundaries or lines of demarcation between ethnic groups are delineated and maintained by certain accepted codes of behaviour governing the social interaction between such groups [Barth, 1996: 81-82]. Viewed in these terms, the pro-active assertion of its identity by a group vis-à-vis others can be regarded as a form of 'boundary maintenance.' Apart from routine rituals, measures for pro-active boundary maintenance can be triggered off by the concerns of a community that the material and cultural conditions integral to retaining its own

identity are being threatened by the acts of other ethnic groups. It can also be a response to demands imposed upon its members by the nation-state to assimilate with the dominant form of nationalism and national culture.

3. Mohsin [1997: 32], Roy [1995: 54] and Adnan [2004: 39-43]. The Chittagong Hill Tracts Regulation of 1900 (Act 1 of 1900) is known in brief as the CHT Manual or Regulation.
4. Based on revision of the 1961 census data in Adnan [2004: 55-57, Table 4.1].
5. The name of the party can be translated as the Chittagong Hill Tracts People's Solidarity Association.
6. Factors underlying the deterioration in Indo-Bangladesh relations are not presently pursued; however, these issues are discussed elsewhere [Cf. Ali, 1993: 188, and Mohsin, 1997: 167].
7. Based on revised estimates of official census figures, as specified in Table 4.1 and Figure 4.2 of Adnan [2004: 55-57].
8. GoB & PCJSS [1997]. The original treaty is composed in Bengali and its full title can be translated as follows: Accord between the National Committee Concerning the Chittagong Hill Tracts Instituted by the Government of the People's Republic of Bangladesh and the Parbatya Chattagram Jana Samhati Samiti.

References

Adnan, Shapan (2006). 'Ethnicity and Identity in South Asia: Managing the Divide', In Hernaik Singh and Jayan Jose Thomas (eds.), *Engaging South Asia: Challenges and Opportunities,* Singapore: Marshall Cavendish Academic. Proceedings of an International Conference organized by the Institute of South Asian Studies (ISAS), National University of Singapore, held on 28 January 2005.

——(2004). *Migration, Land Alienation and Ethnic Conflict: Causes of Poverty in the Chittagong Hill Tracts of Bangladesh,* Dhaka, Research and Advisory Services.

Ali, S. Mahmud (1993). *The Fearful State: Power, People and Internal War in South Asia,* Zed Books, London.

Barth, Frederik (1996). "Ethnic Groups and Boundaries", Chapter 12 (pp. 75-82) in John Hutchinson and Anthony D. Smith (eds), 1996, *Ethnicity,* Oxford and New York, Oxford University Press.

Bhaumik, S., Guhathakurta, M., and Raychaudhury, S.B. (eds). (1997). *Living on the Edge: Essays on the CHT,* Kathmandu, South Asia Forum for Human Rights.

Bhaumik, Subir (1996). *Insurgent Crossfire: North-East India,* Lancer Publishers and Spantech and Lancer, New Delhi.

Brauns, Claus-Dieter & Loffler, Lorenz G. (1990). *Mru: Hill People on the Border of Bangladesh,* Birkhauser Verlag, Basel, Boston and Berlin.

CHTDP (1987). *Consultant's Final Report: Strengthening of the CHT Development Board and Strengthening of the Agricultural Extension in the CHT,* CHT Development Project (CHTDP), (mimeo).

Dhamai, Binota Moy (2005). *Report of the CHT,* (Circulated by email on 13 June 2005).

Gain, Philip (ed). (1995). *Bangladesh: Land, Forest and Forest People,* Dhaka, Society for Environment and Human Development (SEHD).

GoB & PCJSS (1997). *Accord between the Committee Set Up by the Government of the People's Republic of Bangladesh and the Parbatya Chattogram Jana Samhati Samiti,* Dhaka, 2 December, 1997, (mimeo; in Bengali).

Hazarika, Sanjoy (1994). *Strangers of the Mist: Tales of War and Peace from India's Northeast,* New Delhi, Viking, Penguin Books Ltd.

Hume, Ina (1999). *The Internally Displaced Persons of the CHT, Bangladesh. Case Study 1: Sajek Union; Case Study 2: Farua Union,* Dhaka, (mimeo).

Loffler, L.G. (1991). *Ecology and Human Rights: Two papers on the CHT, Bangladesh, 1991,* Zurich, (mimeo).

Mey, Wolfgang (1984). *Genocide in the Chittagong Hill Tracts, Bangladesh,* IWGIA (International Work Group for Indigenous Affairs), Document No. 51, Copenhagen, IWGIA.

Mohsin, Amena (1997). *The Politics of Nationalism: The Case of the Chittagong Hill Tracts of Bangladesh,* The University Press Limited, Dhaka.

——(1998). "CHT Peace Accord: Looking Ahead", *The Journal of Social Studies,* No. 82, August-October, 1998, pp. 106-117.

PCJSS [Parbatya Chattagram Jana Samhati Samiti] (2002). *JSS' Statement on the Implementation of the 'CHT Accord',* Rangamati,

PCJSS Central Office, Information and Publicity Department, 2 December 2002, 48p, (in Bengali).

——(2004). *Report on the Implementation of the CHT Accord Signed between the Government of Bangladesh and the PCJSS*, Information and Publicity Department, Rangamati, 30 April 2004.

——(2006a). *Communal Attack on Jumma People by Bengali setters at Maischari under Mahalchari in CHT of Bangladesh*, Information and Publicity Department, Rangamati, 9 April 2006.

——(2006b). *Recent Sexual Violence Against Jumma Women in CHT by Military Forces and Bengali Settlers*, Information and Publicity Department, Rangamati, 17 April 2006.

Roy, Raja Devasish (1994). "Land Rights of the Indigenous People of the CHT", *Land*, Vol. 1, No. 1, February, 1994, pp. 11-25, Journal of the Association for Land Reform and Development (ALRD), Dhaka.

——(1995). "Land Rights, Land Use and Indigenous Peoples in the CHT", pp. 49-100, in Philip Gain (ed.), 1995.

——(1996a). *Forests, Forestry and Indigenous People in the CHT, Bangladesh*, Paper Presented at the Workshop on "The Rights of Tribal and Indigenous Peoples", New Delhi, 23-25 February, 1996 (mimeo).

——(1996b). *Decline of Self-Government and Process of Land loss Among the Pahari Adivasis of the CHT: Will this Process lead to Any Change of Direction?* (mimeo; in Bengali).

——(1997a). "Jum (Swidden) Cultivation in the CHT", *Indigenous Affairs*, No. 1, January-March, 1997, IWGIA (International Work Group for Indigenous Affairs), pp. 32-40.

——(1997b). *Legal and Administrative Reforms for the Political Empowerment of Indigenous Peoples in Bangladesh*, Paper presented at the National Adivasi Round Table Conference, Dhaka, 18-20 December, 1997, (mimeo).

——(1997c). "The Population Transfer Programme of 1980s and the Land Rights of the Indigenous Peoples of the CHT," pp. 167-208 in Bhaumik *et al.* (eds), 1997, *Living on the Edge: Essays on the CHT*, Kathmandu, South Asia Forum for Human Rights.

——(1998). *The Accord on the CHT*, TAUNGYA, Rangamati.

Roy, R.C.K. (1996). *Land Rights of the Indigenous Peoples of the CHT*, NORAD/Jumma Peoples Network in Europe (JUPNET).

Shelley, Mizanur Rahman (ed) (1992). *The CHT of Bangladesh: The Untold Story,* Centre for Development Research, Bangladesh (CDRB), Dhaka.

Sopher, David E. (1963). "Population Dislocation in the Chittagong Hills", *The Geographical Review,* Vol. LIII, No. 3, July, 1963, pp. 337-362.

Sopher, David E. (1964). "The Swidden/Wet-Rice Transition Zone in the Chittagong Hills", *Annals of the Association of American Geographers,* Vol. 54, No. 1, March, 1964, pp. 107-126.

van Schendel, Willem (1995). "The Invention of the "Jummas": State Formation and Ethnicity in Southeastern Bangladesh", pp. 121-144 in R. H. Barnes, A. Gray and B. Kingsbury (eds), 1995, *Indigenous Peoples of South Asia,* Association for Asian Studies, Monograph and Occasional Paper Series, Number 48.

4

PAKISTAN'S NATIONAL IDENTITY

ISHTIAQ AHMED

As an ideology and political doctrine, nationalism is a claim set forth on behalf of a body of people claiming to constitute a nation to establish a sovereign state over a specific territory. Once that state comes into being, it has to devise a national identity to distinguish itself from other states. In the case of new or recently established post-colonial states, the construction of a cohesive national identity is imperative. No state can hope to survive in the long run only through the exercise of force or threats. Deeper links in the larger society have to be cultivated so that a substantial number of people, a majority if not the whole of its population, identify with the state in an emotional sense. In order to achieve that, the state has to disseminate the national identity in the larger society through the educational system, the mass media and the political system (Ahmed, 1998).

This is not easily done because the selection of unifying symbols and values is a sensitive matter. There is no absolute or objective criterion (or criteria) on which nationalism in general or state-nationalism in particular can be grounded. Language, religion, common ethnic origin, historical experience, cultural heritage or civilization, common residence in the same region, and various other such factors have been invoked from time to time to construct the national identity. Following Max Weber, I shall employ the ideal type method for classifying state-nationalism in terms of its implications and ramifications for the status and rights of the individuals who constitute its bona fide permanent population. Accordingly, it is argued that all forms of nationalism as well as state-nationalism can be classified as varieties of two analytically distinct types: the civic-political and the cultural/ethnic type of nationalism.

The civic model is conventionally associated with the emancipatory ethos of the European Enlightenment and the French Revolution. It terminated the feudal system of hereditary privileges requiring inferiors to render duties and obligations to superiors. Instead an egalitarian body of equal citizens entitled to equal rights vis-à-vis the state was established in the new dispensation. It took that model another 156 years before it became truly universal and inclusive when the UN Charter of 1945 proclaimed it as the preferred framework for establishing participatory, democratic states. The second type is known as the cultural or ethnic model of nationalism. Its origins are traced to the German Romantic Movement which emerged in reaction to Napoleon's expansionist wars to spread the European Enlightenment's universalism and rationalism to the whole of Europe. For the German patriots it meant hegemony of French culture rather than some universal spread of rationalism. Consequently they emphasized the peculiarity and even uniqueness of German culture. The underlying logic of such theorizing was that nations were organic communities bound together through feelings of affection and solidarity deriving from a sense of common descent and culture. Thus rather than individual citizens being the main bearers of rights it was the nation or community which had priority over members (Brubaker, 1992).

It will be demonstrated below that the Pakistani national identity approximates to the Germanic model, though the founder of Pakistan, Mohammad Ali Jinnah, first used religion to justify the claim to separate statehood for the 'Muslim nation' of India, but then tried to project a vision of inclusive Pakistani nationalism that would grant equal rights to all individuals in the Pakistani population in accordance with the French model of territorial nationalism.

The Controversy over Pakistani National Identity

The creation of Pakistan on 14th August 1947 through a partitioning of colonial India on the basis of contiguous religious majority of Muslims in the north-western and north-eastern zones of the Indian subcontinent was accompanied by the biggest involuntary migration of populations across the international borders that were created between India and Pakistan. While Hindus and Sikhs fled for safety in what became India, Muslims travelled in the opposite direction in search of safe haven. Some 700,000 Hindus, Muslims and Sikhs lost their lives because of the massacres and riots that took place at that time. The All-India Muslim League (henceforth referred to as the Muslim League), which spearheaded the separatist movement for Pakistan had claimed that the Muslims of India were not simply a religious minority; they were a separate and distinct nation on the basis of their Islamic faith and culture. Therefore, it argued that the Muslim nation was entitled to separate statehood. No one articulated this standpoint more eloquently and persuasively than Mohammad Ali Jinnah, the supreme leader of the Muslim League.

However, a notorious ambiguity surrounded the purposes for which Pakistan was created—was it to be simply a national state of Muslims or a theocratic Islamic state based on Shariah (dogmatic Islamic law)? An answer to that question carried direct implications for the rights of non-Muslim minorities. Even in terms of the rights of the various sections of the Muslim population, there was a problem about the rights of women and various minority Muslim sects. Jinnah had never provided any clear answer to this question. In many of his formal statements he drew the contours of a modern Muslim state but also gave assurances to the religious elite that the Shariah would be applicable to Muslims (*Constituent Assembly Debates*, 1949: 46).

For Pakistani Muslims, especially those who had either been victims or active participants in the partition riots, there could be little doubt that Pakistan had been specifically established for the Muslim nation. The Muslim League had invoked Islam to mobilize all sections of Muslim society. Sectarian and doctrinal differences were cleverly ignored and emphasis was laid on Islam as common culture and identity. Thus all categories of Muslims who identified themselves as Muslims in the census records rallied to the call of the Muslim League for the creation of a Muslim polity. Not surprisingly they nurtured diverse interests, hopes and visions with its establishment. One can sum up the variegated ideas about Pakistan in the following words:

> Pakistan meant different things to different people. To the landlords it meant continued leadership, to the doctrinal-minded Muslims, a unique opportunity to create an Islamic state in the light of their ideas: to the Muslim intelligentsia and the poorer classes, a state where social and economic justice would prevail and their dignity established, according to Iqbalite teachings; to the peasants, freedom from the yoke of the Hindu money-lender; to the regional leaders, a greater autonomy than was expected in a united India dominated by Congress; to the Muslim bourgeoisie, the necessary environment where they could develop their potential...; and to bureaucrats and the military, an excellent opportunity to secure quick promotions; and to the military establishment it brought a central role in a country where the civilian political process was dependent from the very beginning upon its support and active participation (Ahmed, 1987: 80-1).

It should be noted that after Pakistan became independent, the hopes of the masses that radical economic reforms would be undertaken to liberate them from abject poverty remained largely unfulfilled. The most dramatic change was, of course, the remission of all debts to Hindu moneylenders. On the other hand, dependence and subordination to the Muslim landlords continued as before. Such difficulties were compounded further by the fact that neither in the West Pakistani provinces

(Baluchistan, North-West Frontier Province, Punjab and Sindh) nor in East Pakistan was there any significant industrial development. Moreover, education levels were very low and the overall social development was poor. Rich landlords, a miniscule commercial bourgeoisie, a small intelligentsia and the vast majority made up of millions of peasants, artisans and other types of poor people constituted the social pyramid of Pakistani society. The crucial broad-based and educated middle-class that could help provide a strong social base for a secular type of democracy was conspicuous by its absence.

Moreover, the movement for Pakistan was essentially negative in its orientation: it had come into being in opposition to a perceived fear that in a united India the Hindu majority would be a permanent political majority thus reducing Muslims to the position of second-class citizens. Such complications were aggravated by the fact that Pakistan came into being in the very last months of the colonial period, when negotiations between the Muslim League and the Indian National Congress mediated by the British failed to find a power-sharing formula that could keep India united. These difficulties were compounded further by the fact that the Muslim League was a loose collection of Muslim politicians with regional support bases. It did not represent a cohesive or coherent political party with grassroots organizations throughout the country (Ahmed, 1987: 77-80).

Under the circumstances, the civil service and the military came to dominate the state. The type of government that has dominated Pakistan has been described as the vice-regal system where bureaucrats and the military establishment have subordinated the representatives from civil society, including those elected by the people (Talbot, 1998: 54). Since Pakistani independence, the military-bureaucratic oligarchy has stepped in several times dismissing sitting governments on charges of corruption, inefficiency or the breakdown of law and order. While this oligarchy has preferred an authoritarian type of political order, in terms of national identity, however, the elite have shown no clear vision. Over time, however, the religious type of national identity has strengthened and acquired fundamentalist trappings.

The Modernist Phase. The first authoritative statement on national identity made on 11 August 1947 by Mohammad Ali Jinnah surprised many because in it he reverted to his earlier moorings of constitutionalism and democracy. Among other things, he observed the following in a long address:

> You are free; you are free to go to your temples, you are free to go to your mosques or to any other place of worship in this State of Pakistan. You may belong to any religion or caste or creed–that has nothing to do with the business of the State.... We are starting with this fundamental principle that we are all citizens and equal citizens of one State... I think we should keep that in front of us as our ideal and you will find that in due course Hindus would cease to be Hindus and Muslims would cease to be Muslims, not in the religious sense, because that is the personal faith of each individual, but in the political sense as citizens of the State (*Speeches and Writings of Mr Jinnah,* 1976: 403-4).

This patently secular and territorial idea of nation has generated unending controversy subsequently. While the fundamentalists usually dismiss it as irrelevant and an aberration, moderates argue that Jinnah was actually operating within an ideal Islamic framework of tolerance and justice for non-Muslims within an Islamic state (Shah 1998). Marginalized secularists, leftists and oppressed minorities, however, raise it to the level of a sacred covenant that his successors have allegedly broken. Whatever the motivation for the speech it is doubtful whether in the wake of the communal riots such a prescription enjoyed any real credibility in Muslim-Pakistani society. After his death on 11th September 1948, the idea of a secular state never again received much attention in Pakistani politics. Rather, Islamic idiom became a central feature of official rhetoric. It is interesting to note that in an official collection of the speeches of Jinnah published by the Research Society of Pakistan in 1966, his 11 August 1947 speech was omitted altogether (*Selected Speeches,* 1966)

One can even argue that once the initial euphoria was over and a framework for national identity and state building had to be found, the Pakistani leadership felt constrained to distinguish itself from India. Pakistan had been won in the name of religious nationalism. There were undoubtedly other issues to be dealt with by the government of Prime Minister Liaqat Ali Khan (assassinated 16 October, 1951), but maintaining distinctiveness from Congress and secular India must have been an important consideration. Thus the Objectives Resolution moved in the Pakistan Constituent Assembly by Khan on 7 March 1949 proclaimed the novel idea that sovereignty over the entire universe belonged to God. Democracy was to be practised, but within 'Islamic limits'. The minorities were assured that their legitimate interests would be safeguarded and that provisions would be made for them, in accordance with Islam, to freely profess and practise their religions and cultures (*Constituent Assembly Debates,* 1949:1-2). Such proclamations sounded pompous and decorative rather than substantive, but in the long run they proved to be a source of legitimation for the Islamization of Pakistan.

Thus the first constitution of Pakistan adopted in 1956 contained a commitment to bringing all laws into conformity with Islam. It could not be put into operation because the government was overthrown by a military coup in October 1958. The second constitution given in 1962 by General Mohammad Ayub Khan reiterated the commitment to bring all laws in conformity with Islam. The third constitution adopted by the National Assembly of Pakistan in 1973 took further steps towards Islamization. Unlike the first two constitutions that only required the president of the republic to be a Muslim, the third required the prime minister to be a Muslim too. It further obliged both of them to take an oath testifying their belief in the finality of Prophet Muhammad's mission (*Constitution of the Islamic Republic of Pakistan,* 1975).

In 1974 the National Assembly declared the Ahmadiyya sect as non-Muslim. The initiator, ironically, of this change was Prime Minister Zulfikar Ali Bhutto (1971-77), a man generally considered a left-leaning politician. Bhutto possibly sought to capture the political initiative from the clerics by pre-empting their favourite demand that Ahmadis be declared as non-Muslims. This proved to be a colossal miscalculation on his part because it only emboldened the fundamentalists to demand greater compliance with their programme of Islamization. In 1977 Bhutto was overthrown after a prolonged nationwide campaign against him by the combined opposition parties who accused him of maintaining an authoritarian and vindictive government. The military took over. General Muhammad Zia-ul-Haq was a committed fundamentalist.

Fundamentalism in the Periphery

A movement in favour of a fundamentalist polity enjoyed favour with many clerics from the very beginning of the creation of Pakistan. One can define Islamic fundamentalism as an anti-modern, anti-democratic, violence-prone ideological-political movement. It invariably refers to an attitude idealizing the polity created by the Prophet Muhammad in the 7th century. The Sunni consider the period of his immediate four successors, the pious caliphs, as a continuation of that ideal state and seek to emulate it. The Shias reduce that period even more and celebrate only the period of the fourth caliph Ali who they consider as the only legitimate successor of Muhammad. The ideal of a perfect Islamic state has fascinated Muslims throughout history (Ahmed, 1987). Until 1977, however, the fundamentalists in Pakistan remained alienated from positions of authority, and it was the Westernized elite which ruled. Nevertheless, the fundamentalists continued to put forth their agenda in different ways.

The ideologue of such a movement was Abul Ala Maududi, the leader of the Jama'at-e-Islami. In 1951 he compiled a 22-point political programme which sought a thorough Islamization of Pakistan. He interpreted the notion of sovereignty of God to mean that the Shariah would apply to all sectors of life within the Islamic polity as well as to relations with non-Muslim states and societies. Although the government was to be formed through elections as in Western democracies, female equality and equal rights for non-Muslims were rejected. He was able to secure the signatures of the leading Sunni (of the various orthodox orientations) and Shia clerics to that document (Maududi, 1980: 332-336).

In external matters too, Maududi wanted classical Islamic ideas of Dar-ul-Islam (abode of peace where Islamic law applies) and Dar-ul-Harb (enemy territory) to be observed by the state. It meant that the Islamic state could establish peace with its neighbours through treaty but in the ultimate sense no real peace could be consolidated between the world of Islam and non-Muslims (Maududi, 1981). The first major outburst of a fundamentalist type of politics took place when the mainly Sunni clerics began a campaign in 1953 to have the Ahmadiyya sect declared non-Muslim.

The Anti-Ahmadiyya Riots of 1953. The controversy had its origins in the claims of Mirza Ghulam Ahmad (1835-1908), born at Qadian in the Punjab, to being a prophet. In addition he made statements which were seen by other Muslims as openly pro-British and against the Muslim community; most notably his rejection of jihad (holy war) against the British. After his death the Ahmadiyya movement went through a period of internal rift and conflict. During the colonial period the Ahmadis received government protection. They were able to win some converts in Punjab. Some prominent Ahmadis, among whom Sir Muhammad Zafrulla Khan was the most well-known, played a leading role in the struggle for the creation of Pakistan. Sir Zafrulla was subsequently appointed as the first foreign minister of Pakistan by Jinnah. It was widely believed that Ahmadi officers in the army and the civil service were using their influence to convert people to their faith in Pakistan (*Court of Inquiry Report* 1954).

In 1953 a violent agitation broke out in Punjab against the Ahmadis. During this agitation, many Ahmadis were killed and the looting of their property was widespread. The agitation was crushed following the imposition of martial law by the central government. The Court of Inquiry for the riots, headed by two judges of the Lahore High Court, found that not only clerics but also leading figures of the Muslim League provincial government in Punjab were involved in the violence. In the report they warned of the consequences of exploiting Islam for political purposes and described the Islamic state model of the clerics as an obscurantist and oppressive one (*Court of Inquiry Report* 1954).

Fundamentalism as State Ideology. The growth and ascent of a fundamentalist political jargon in Pakistani politics can be traced to lay politicians, whether in the government or outside it, who found it a convenient ploy to outbid each other in asserting their own piety and patriotism, while accusing others of being renegades to Islam and agents of hostile foreign powers. In cumulative terms, such a propensity invariably benefited the fundamentalist lobby since the employment of Islamic terminology meant borrowing it from fundamentalist sources and authority. From the mid-1960s onwards, as class struggles and regional conflicts greatly increased in Pakistan, Maududi's version of an Islamic state appeared as formidable counterweight that could be wielded against the emerging radical threats. He and some military officers began to argue that an ideology of Pakistan based on Islam existed and through an ordinance issued by the military government of General Yayha Khan in 1969, Islam was declared exclusively as the ideology of Pakistan (Ahmed, 1999: 230).

With the coming into power of General Zia in 1977, an unabashed champion of fundamentalism was now in power. He succinctly declared his political mission: 'I consider the establishment of an Islamic order a *prerequisite* for the country.' (Noman 1988: 118). In 1979 the government announced the imposition of the Hudud Ordinance i.e. punishments laid down in the Quran and Sunna for the offences of adultery (death by stoning), fornication (100 lashes), false accusation of adultery (80 lashes), drinking alcohol (80 lashes), theft (cutting off the right hand), highway robbery (when the offence is only robbery, cutting off hands and feet, for robbery with murder, death either by the sword or crucifixion) (Ahmed, 1999: 231).

In 1983-84, further legal restrictions were imposed on the Ahmadis who were forbidden to use Islamic nomenclature for their worship, places of worship and so on. In 1984, a new Law of Evidence was adopted which reduced the value of the evidence of a female witness to half that of a male witness in a court of law. In 1985, a Shariat bill was moved in the national assembly by two members of the Jamaat-e-Islami that sought to establish the supremacy of the Quran and Sunna in a substantial manner. Sunni-Hanafi interpretations of puritan Ulama (Deobandi usually) were to be the standard norm and practice. Most central to the bill was the creation of Shariat Courts. Hudud offences were to be within the exclusive jurisdiction of the Shariat Courts (Ahmed, 1999: 231). In 1986, a Blasphemy Law was introduced under Section 295-C of the Penal Code. According to the law, the use of derogatory remarks with respect to the Holy Prophet, whether by words, either spoken or written, or by visible representation, or by any imputation, innuendo or insinuation, directly or indirectly, would be punishable with either death, imprisonment for life, or a fine (Ahmed, 2005: 203).

Women, non-Muslims and minority sects. The so-called 'Islamization' of the Pakistani legal code institutionalized discrimination against women, non-Muslims and deviant sects, thereby reducing them to the position of second-rate citizens. Thus for example, when it came to rape, women were hugely disadvantaged by the *Zina* Ordinance introduced by General Zia. It is interesting to note that rape as sexual intercourse forced upon a woman is not recognized in the Quran, but it was acknowledged by Muslim jurists as *zina bil jabr* or sexual intercourse under duress. Under the Pakistan Penal Code (PPC) Section 375 inherited from the colonial system the evidence given by the victim was accepted. Under the new law, the evidence of the victim was not admitted, nor was that of any other woman. Moreover PPC Section 375 had protected girls under fourteen by providing that even with their consent, sexual intercourse with them would constitute rape (Mehdi, 1994: 123). This immunity was not included in the *Zina* Ordinance. The traditional Islamic Law of Evidence pertaining to *zina bil jabr* was that four male witnesses had to testify under oath that they actually saw the penetration of the woman's vagina by the rapist. Furthermore, under Islamic law, if the rape was not proved, the woman accusing someone of rape could be punished severely on charges of false accusation of rape. Under *hadood* law the punishment was 100 lashes. In subsequent years, many rape victims were severely punished because they could not provide the required evidence of four pious male witnesses (Jahangir and Jilani, 2003).

Besides such harsh misogynist laws, more concrete social measures were undertaken to impose a chaste code of conduct for women. In 1980, a circular was issued to all government offices that prescribed a proper Muslim dress for female employees. Wearing of a chador (loose cloth covering one's head) was made obligatory. A campaign to eliminate obscenity and pornography was also announced. This however took the form of a campaign against the general emancipation and equal rights for women. Leading Muslim theologians notorious for their misogynist prejudices against female emancipation were brought on national television to justify the various restrictions and limitations on the freedom of women (Ahmed, 1999: 232). As the general situation of women deteriorated, some educated women in urban centres such as Lahore, Karachi and Islamabad began to agitate and demonstrate. Police repression followed immediately. The succeeding governments of Benazir Bhutto (1988-90, 1994-96), Nawaz Sharif (1990-93; 1997-99) did not dare to remove the laws against women, imposed during the Zia era.

Until 1977, although various restrictions existed on the political rights of non-Muslims, they were more symbolic than substantial. Zia introduced separate electorates for non-Muslims in 1985. Non-Muslim voters were not to vote in the general elections for general seats, but only for non-Muslim candidates. Since then, many individuals, mostly Christians and Ahmadis, have been charged with blasphemy. The death sentence has been passed at the lower levels but commuted to lighter sentences at the higher level. Nevertheless a number of individuals set free by the courts have subsequently been murdered by assailants suspected of belonging to various extremist groups. In October 1997, a retired high court judge Arif Bhatti was shot dead by gunmen believed to belong to extremist groups, apparently because he had acquitted two Christians charged with blasphemy (Ahmed, 2002: 57-89).

Since the 1990s, the perennial sectarian tension between the Sunni majority and the substantial Shia minority (some 15-20 per cent) has taken the shape of terrorist attacks between armed militias of the two sides. The coming into power of the Shia Imam, Ayutollah Khomeini in 1979 in Iran, and the reaction of Iran's Sunni Arab neighbours to it, resulted in the clandestine supply of large sums of money, leaflets, books, audio and video cassette-tapes and other means to propagate one point of view or the other in Pakistan. In addition to regular gun-battles, bomb-attacks and assassinations targeting rival Sunni and Shia Ulama and activists, innocent worshippers in mosques of rival sects have also been pitilessly gunned down (Ahmed 1998: 208-209).

Pakistan Delinks from Militant Islam

On 12 October 1999, General Pervez Musharraf overthrew the elected government of Nawaz Sharif, and declared himself first as the chief executive and later as the president of Pakistan. On 11 September 2001, a group of terrorists believed to be members of the Al-Qaeda movement led by a veteran of the Afghan jihad, the Saudi, Osama bin Laden, hijacked civilian aircraft in various US cities and flew them into the World Trade Center and the Pentagon. Following the monumental attacks that killed several thousand people, the US rapidly mustered its armed forces and established an anti-terrorist coalition. The pressure placed on Pakistan to choose sides at the time led to a decisive move by Musharraf to unlink his administration from the various Pakistani fundamentalist militant outfits, while agreeing to open up Pakistani airspace, port facilities and even allowing the Americans to establish bases in Pakistan.

On 1 October and 13 December 2001, militants carried out terrorist attacks on the Kashmir Assembly in Srinagar, the capital of the India-administered Kashmir, and the Indian Parliament in Delhi, respectively. India responded by mobilising its troops along the 2900 kilometres India-Pakistan border and the line of control in Kashmir. Pakistan followed suit. Given that both India and Pakistan had demonstrated their ability to explode nuclear devices in 1998 and had engaged in the Kargil conflict in May 1999, there was widespread concern of the possibility that nuclear weapons could be used by the adversaries if the border-standoff escalated into open conflict.

International concern and pressure increased enormously on the two states to withdraw from their standoff. India, however, refused to do that as long as Pakistan supported what it described as cross-border terrorism. The US, Britain and other Western powers backed the Indian demand for Pakistan to forgo its support to militant groups. Consequently, in an address to the Pakistani nation on 12 January 2002, General Pervez Musharraf publically dissociated himself from fundamentalist tendencies and movements. He described Pakistan as a modern Islamic state based on a moderate, tolerant interpretation of Islam (Musharraf, 2002). Later in an address to Muslim clerics he spoke about a middle path, a tolerant non-divisive approach to Islam (Musharraf, 18 January, 2002). Most significantly he abolished the system of separate electorates whereby non-Muslims were required to vote separately from the Muslims, and the law on rape was changed so that the requirement of four pious male witnesses was not required to establish the offence. The testimony of the victim has also come to be admitted as valid.

In subsequent clarifications, however, Musharraf dispelled speculations that Pakistan might become a secular state. He reiterated that Pakistan will remain an Islamic Republic. For example, when on 14 February 2002 the US House of Representative passed a resolution urging Pakistan to abolish the blasphemy laws and the ban on the Ahmadiyya sect to call themselves Muslims, the Pakistan government refused to comply. It stated that the Hudud and Blasphemy laws were an intrinsic part of the Pakistani constitution and would remain in force although measures would be taken to see to it that were not employed in an arbitrary manner (Kamran, 2002).

Such vacillation between moderate and fundamentalist types of Islam has not helped Musharraf attain a consensus on national identity. On the contrary, the close relationship with the United States that he cultivated after the 9/11 terrorists attacks have greatly angered the fundamentalists who, in turn, have declared a holy war on the Musharraf regime. The result has been several armed conflicts between the Pakistan Army and the fundamentalists. Hundreds of deaths, including those of innocent people have taken place as a result of terrorist bomb blasts and the government bombardment of fundamentalist strongholds in the tribal areas on the border with Afghanistan.

Conclusion

There can be little doubt that Pakistani state-nationalism derives from the Germanic type of cultural nationalism. Since Pakistan had been created in the name of Muslim nationalism, its national identity was inextricably bound to that cultural factor. Soon after independence, the ruling elite in Pakistan decided to include Islam in the elaboration of national identity. Such an elite ruled in the vice-regal authoritarian tradition. The distinction between Muslim (cultural) and Islamic (religious) being rather blurred in the Muslim heritage, the constitutional and legal frameworks began to borrow terminology and jargon from classical Islamic political theory.

The coming into power of General Muhammad Zia-ul-Haq in 1977 placed fundamentalist forces directly at the helm of affairs in Pakistan. He strove to Islamize Pakistani national identity in line with fundamentalist ideology. This resulted in various discriminatory laws being introduced in Pakistan. After 9/11, however, the Pakistani regime has moved away considerably from fundamentalism, as is evident in Musharraf's assertion that Pakistan will be a modern, moderate, tolerant Islamic state. Such vacillations between moderate and fundamentalist types of Islam however make it very difficult to place Pakistan on an ideological continuum with the theocratic and secular states being at the opposite ends of the spectrum. Under all circumstances, however, Pakistan as an Islamic state–moderate or fundamentalist–constitutionally and legally discriminates between the primary

Pakistani nation constituted by Muslims, or rather by Muslim men, and other categories of lesser citizens. Women of all categories, non-Muslims and 'deviant' sects are subjected to legal and constitutional-disadvantages. Consequently its national identity is exclusive as it does not include all the bona fide permanent residents of Pakistan as equal citizens of the state.

References

Ahmed, Ishtiaq (1987). *The Concept of an Islamic State: An Analysis of the Ideological Controversy in Pakistan.* London: Frances Pinter; New York: St. Martin's Press.

——(1998). *State, Nation and Ethnicity in Contemporary South Asia.* London and New York: Pinter Publishers.

——(1999). 'South Asia' in David Westerlund and Ingvar Svanberg (eds), *Islam Outside the Arab World.* Richmond: Curzon.

——(2002). 'Globalisation and Human Rights in Pakistan' in *International Journal of Punjab Studies,* Vol. 9, No. 1.

——(2005). 'The Politics of Group Rights in India and Pakistan' in Ishtiaq Ahmed (ed.), *The Politics of Group Rights.* Lanham/Boulder/New York/Toronto/Oxford: University Press of America.

Brubaker, Rogers (1992). *Citizenship and Nationalism in France and Germany.* London and Cambridge, Massachusetts: Harvard University Press.

Jahangir, A. and Jilani, H. (2003). *The Hudood Ordinances: A Divine Sanction?* Lahore: Sang-e-Meel Publications.

Kamran, Mohammad (2002). 'Blasphemy Law, Hudood Ord to stay' in Daily Times, Lahore, 25 May 2002, Daily News, *http://www.dailytimes.com.pk/default.asp?page=story_25-5-2002.*

Maududi, Abul Ala (1980). *The Islamic Law and Constitution.* Lahore: Islamic Publications Ltd.

——(1981). *Al-Jihad Fi al-Islam.* Lahore: Idara Tarjuman-ul-Quran.

Mehdi, R. (1994). *The Islamization of the Law in Pakistan.* Richmond, UK: Curzon Press.

Musharraf, Pervez (2002). Address to the Nation, *http://www.pak.gov.pk/public/President_address.htm,* 12 January.

Musharraf, Pervez (2002). Address to the Ulema and Mashaikh, *http://www.pak.gov.pk/public/President_address.htm,* 18 January.

Noman, Omar (1988). *The Political Economy of Pakistan.* London and New York: KPI.

Research Society of Pakistan (1966). *Selected Speeches and Statements of the Quaid-i-Azam Mohammad Ali Jinnah.* Lahore: Research Society of Pakistan.

Shah, Dr. Nasim Hasan (1998). 'The Myth of Jinnah's belief in Secularism', in *Dawn* (Internet Edition), 14 August.

Sh. Muhammad Ashraf (1976). *Speeches and Writings of Mr. Jinnah, Vol. II.* Lahore: Sh. Muhammad Ashraf: Lahore.

Talbot, Ian (1998). *Pakistan: A Modern History.* London: Hurst & Company.

The Government of Pakistan (1949). *The Constituent Assembly of Pakistan Debates,* Volume 5. Karachi: Government of Pakistan Publications.

——(1975). *The Constitution of the Islamic Republic of Pakistan* Lahore: Publishers United Ltd.

——(1954). *Report of the Court of Inquiry Constituted under Punjab Act II of 1954 to Enquire into the Punjab Disturbances of 1953* (also known as Munir Report), Lahore: Government Printing Press.

5

THE KHALISTAN MOVEMENT IN INDIA: THE INTERPLAY OF POLITICS AND STATE POWER

Rajshree Jetly

This paper postulates that the course of any separatist movement is contingent on a variety of factors. First, the nature of the movement itself: its leadership, organisational base, numerical strength and the historical and cultural forces which lend character and weight to the movement. Second, the response of governments to ethnic groups: the strategies employed by them *vis-à-vis* the respective groups-coercion, conciliation or a blend of the two, and the socio-political and economic policies of the state towards them. Third, the level of external support provided by other countries to the groups in question, the role of the diaspora in sustaining the movement from outside, and the role of other organisations in providing arms and other forms of support to the groups.

If all the above are present-that is, the ethnic group is well organised and has a strong leadership base, the response of the state is repressive, and the group finds external support in the form of arms and finance-there is a greater possibility of the group moving towards a separate state. Conversely the absence of any one or more of these factors makes it extremely difficult for a separatist movement to succeed, as witnessed in the rise and decline of separatism in Punjab.

Background to the Khalistan Movement

Sikhs constitute less than two per cent of the population of India and form a small minority group in the country. Most Indian Sikhs are concentrated in the state of Punjab, situated on the North-western border of India. In spite of being a small minority, they are more than well-represented in Indian business, the army and the bureaucracy. In addition, going by all socio-economic indicators, Punjab is clearly one of the most prosperous states of India, with relatively high literacy rates and one of the highest per capita incomes in the country. Notwithstanding this, Punjab witnessed the alienation of a large number of Sikhs in the 1980s with the Sikh quest for a separate identity revolving around two important symbols: language (Punjabi) and religion (Sikhism). These were used to emphasise their distinctiveness in relation to Hindi-speaking groups and Hindu regions such as the neighbouring state of Haryana, and to press for more economic and political privileges from the central government.

The period prior to the partition of the subcontinent in 1947 provides some insight into the politicisation of the Sikh identity and their subsequent disillusionment with the Indian state in the post-partition period. Sikhs had proven their loyalty to the British in the early years of British rule in Punjab, particularly as members of the British Indian Army. However, their loyalty to British rule was clearly on the wane after the Rowlatt Act (1919), which gave the colonial government sweeping powers to incarcerate people without trial to maintain internal order. Protests against the Act met with a stiff response from colonial authorities, the most significant of which was the Jallianwala Bagh massacre on 13 April 1919 which effectively turned many Sikhs against the British. Their anger deepened when instead of the much-promised 33 per cent representation that they expected as reward for their services in the army, they were given, under the Government of India Act 1919, only 15 out of a total of 93 seats in the Punjab legislative council. (Khwaja, 1980:

204). The Ramsay McDonald award of April 1932 which established separate electorates for minorities also deprived the Sikhs of their rightful representation based on their percentage. (K Singh, 1991: 232).

Sikh leaders had wanted the creation of a Sikh state along the lines of Pakistan. However, the Muslim League that had fought for the creation of Pakistan had enjoyed a political advantage at the time, and the number of Sikhs was no where close to the number of Muslims (there were 5,500,000 Sikhs as compared to 90,000,000 Muslims at that time). Further, the Sikhs were not concentrated in any area which could be carved out into a separate state. Under the circumstances, the Sikhs reluctantly agreed to the partition of Punjab in 1947 resulting in the western districts of the state, which had a Muslim majority, becoming part of Pakistan while the eastern districts of Punjab that had a Sikh-Hindu majority remaining as part of the Indian state.

Demand for a separate state. The Partition of Punjab however did not mark the end of aspirations amongst some Sikh groups for a Sikh homeland. Initiatives such as Patiala and East Punjab States Union (PEPSU) in 1948 and moves for a Punjabi Suba from the 1950s onwards sustained this desire. The Indian government, however, was not prepared to create a state based on religious grounds, although in 1966, it conceded to dividing Punjab on 'linguistic' lines into Punjab and Haryana. The former, with a Sikh majority espoused the Punjabi language, while the latter, with a Hindu majority, emphasised Hindi (M. Singh, 1988:165).

The creation of the Punjabi state did not, however, completely satisfy the demands of the Sikhs. In the new Punjab, Sikhs formed approximately 54 per cent of the population. Punjabi was declared the official language but the situation remained complicated because a large number of Hindus continued to reside in Punjab and showed little enthusiasm for Punjabi. The retention of Chandigarh as a union territory serving as capital for both Punjab and Haryana, and the perceived unfair distribution of river waters further instilled a sense of discrimination among the Sikhs.

Party politics in Punjab. Sikh resentment was also intensified by the regular tussle between the Congress and the Akali Party to capture power in Punjab. Following Indian independence, the Akali Dal representing the interests of the Sikhs, and the Congress Party were the two major political forces in Punjab that alternately shared power in the state. The dilemma for the Akali party was that despite being a strong advocate of the Sikh culture and religion, it never enjoyed the full support of the Sikhs. Its narrow support base comprised the Jat Sikhs and segments of the urban Sikh population. Its rival, the Congress party, had been more effective in state politics, relying on Hindus, scheduled castes[1], and segments of the non-scheduled caste rural Sikh population.

Subsequently the Akali Dal failed to capitalise on its advantage of being the sole and effective champion of the Sikhs (Kaur, 1999: 61-69). It was also plagued by internal squabbles which intensified by the early 1980s.

Further, the Congress party under Mrs Gandhi, played a significant role in undermining the Akali Dal (Kothari and Deshingkar, 1985: 623-24). Mrs Gandhi adopted a highly authoritarian approach with an aggressive agenda of centralisation, which in 1980 saw nine states, whose governments were unfavourable to the policies of the central government, placed under temporary President's rule. Punjab was one of these states where the Akali Dal and Janata Sangh combine was dismissed. In order to split the electorate and ensure that the Akali Dal did not garner widespread support, Congress cultivated the religious leader Jarnail Singh Bhindranwale as an alternative power base.

Bhindranwale, a young Sikh religious preacher with a flair for oratory, was a natural rallying point for those inclined to a more assertive brand of politics. It is widely accepted that Giani Zail Singh, the former President of India and trusted aide of Mrs Gandhi, was instrumental in bringing Bhindranwale into the political limelight. (K Singh, 1991:332) In the 1978-79 elections of the Shiromani Gurudwara Prabahandak Committee (SGPC)-the council in charge of Sikh holy shrines-the Congress government supported the extremists, including

Bhindranwale's nominees, against the Akali Dal. (Tully and Jacob, 1985: 57-83).

According to Atul Kohli,

> The repeated failure of the Akalis to wrest power from Congress had left open a political space for those who argued that increased militancy was the only means for protecting Sikh interests. Bhindrawale stepped into that space. (1990: 361).

Bhindranwale was initially Congress's master stroke as he put the Akali party under considerable pressure. However, as Bhindranwale's popularity grew, both the Akali Dal and Congress found themselves in a dilemma. Supporting Bhindranwale gave both parties some mileage with respect to the Sikh voters but risked alienating Hindu voters. Bhindranwale was very quick to read the signs and had the political acumen to capitalise on this situation by playing the two parties off against each other. Congress soon found that the genie it had unleashed was refusing to go back in its bottle.

The Anandpur Sahib Resolution. The Akali found themselves being pushed into a corner when the Congress government at the centre raised the spectre of Sikh separatism to exploit the insecurity of Hindu voters. Concerned with their declining popularity, lack of solidarity in the rank and file of the party, and the machinations of the Congress to oust them from power, the Akali brought out the Anandpur Sahib Resolution in 1978. (G Singh, 1991: 258-67). This declaration addressed the economic concerns of the Punjab along with the religious and ethnic demands of the Sikhs. The resolution was not secessionist in content but called for greater autonomy for Punjab and protection of the cultural and religious rights of the Sikhs.

The resolution also demanded that Punjab be given full jurisdiction over its administration and law, and that the power of the central government be restricted to the management of foreign policy, defence, currency, and general communications. In addition, two issues that came to the fore of the political agenda of the Akalis, were the transfer of Chandigarh to Punjab in lieu of the two Hindi speaking villages of Abohar and Fazilka in Punjab to Haryana, and the re-distribution of river waters that would favour Punjab. The Chandigarh issue had long been a bone of contention between the federal government and the states of Punjab and Haryana. Not willing to forego the Hindu votes from the state of Haryana, Prime minister, Indira Gandhi declared that Chandigarh would go to Punjab provided Haryana was suitably compensated and got its share of Hindi-speaking areas in Punjab. (White Paper on the Punjab Agitation, 1984:15). But this was complicated because Abohar and Fazilka were situated in the heartland of Punjab and giving them to Haryana entailed the construction of a corridor between the two states. The inability to reach an acceptable solution resulted in Chandigarh remaining as the joint capital of Punjab and Haryana, thereby exacerbating resentment among Sikhs in Punjab.

Similarly, the Sikhs' long-held grievance against the federal government had been that the water from the three rivers, Ravi, Beas and Sutlej flowed through Punjab but an elaborate canal system diverted water to irrigate drier areas of other states like Haryana and Rajasthan. In the wake of the *Punjab Reorganisation Act* of 1966, the central government announced that Punjab would get only 23 per cent of the water from its rivers while the rest would go to Rajasthan and Haryana states. Even though their share went up subsequently from 23 to 24 per cent, the Akalis felt that this was insufficient. The matter was referred to a tribunal for a final decision which never came, leaving Sikhs in a state of dissatisfaction over an issue which was seen as critical to agricultural growth and development in the state.

Economic Dimensions. The political factors, as discussed above, laid the basis for the crystallisation of Sikh identity but the economic factors also added to a deepening sense of alienation and growth of separatist sentiments among the Sikhs. Punjab is the fourth smallest state in India and accounts for nearly 2.5 per cent of its population. It is, however, one of India's most prosperous states. For instance, in 1985-86, per capita income in the state was Rs. 1,600 compared to an all-India average of Rs. 779 at 1970-71 prices. (Gill, 1988: 437)

Similarly, although 72 per cent of its people lived in rural areas, Punjab's percentage of rural people living below the poverty line was the lowest among all Indian states and it had the highest average life expectancy. From the mid 1960s onwards following the Green Revolution, Punjab made spectacular strides in terms of agricultural productivity and emerged as the bread basket of India, producing one-fourth of the total wheat in the country, apart from being a major producer of cereals such as rice, maize, millets, and cash crops such as cotton, sugarcane and groundnuts.

However, Punjab's relative wealth and prosperity could not contain the popular disaffection against the centre for a number of reasons. The gains from the Green Revolution were distributed unequally among the various sections of society and the different regions in Punjab. This led to the growing pauperisation of marginal and poor peasants, who could neither reap the benefits of the land nor find employment in the industrial sector (G. Singh, 1984: 42-43). The Green Revolution was successful initially because the government had provided subsidies and support prices to help the farmers. However, this could not continue indefinitely and with the rising cost of fertilisers and pesticides, small farmers were the worst hit, accumulating huge losses and debts. Even big landlords who could avail themselves of credit facilities at cheap rates, began to feel the pinch with the increase in the prices of inputs, and shortages of electricity and water. Also, while increase in productivity was the main objective of the Green Revolution, productivity could not be sustained for long because the new varieties had generated a new ecological vulnerability by reducing genetic diversity and affecting soil and water systems.

Ironically, the rise of prosperity in Punjab was accompanied by growing unemployment. While agriculture witnessed considerable growth, the industrial infrastructure of the state remained relatively under-developed save for some small-scale industries such as woollen textiles and hosiery financed largely by the remittances of overseas Sikhs. Many Punjabi youths were forced to go elsewhere to seek employment and, in turn, Punjab attracted semi-skilled and unskilled labour from states like Bihar and Uttar Pradesh. All this led to growing resentment among many sections of society, fuelling wide discontent among the masses. The status conferred by the green revolution on Punjab, as the breadbasket of India became a cause for discontent, when the benefits started fading.

The situation was aggravated by perceived injustices in the distribution of wealth and opportunities. Sikh farmers and peasants felt that they were not getting their due and that much of the benefits from their efforts were flowing to other parts of the country. The mismanagement of the wealth generated from the Green Revolution as well as the failure to develop other industries to absorb educated Sikh youth added fuel to the fire. It is important to note, however, that the economic factors worked only as an add-on to growing political discontent (Gupta, 1996:70). In other words, even though economic grievances were emphasised time and again to point to discrimination at the hands of the centre, they only gained credence once the political situation had deteriorated and the secessionist demand had become more viable. This explains why the tapering off of the green revolution in the mid 1970s was not followed by militancy or demands for separatism, which became a feature of Punjab's politics only at the beginning of the 1980s.

Growth of Religious identity. The economic and political crisis began to take religious overtones when the Akali Dal, the main party of the Jat Sikhs or the farmers, started couching its economic and social demands in the name of religion. This laid the basis for militancy in Punjab. The rise of Sikh fundamentalism can be traced back to 1978 when Bhindranwale assumed the role of a religious preacher and leader in the Sikh community. As the central government failed to reach a political settlement with the Akali party on issues such as the capital territory of Punjab and the distribution of river waters, the stature of Bhindranwale went from strength to strength; Bhindranwale directed his anger at the central government and started advocating ways of propogating his brand of Sikhism which he claimed would purge religious malpractices that had crept into the order over the years. His messages were carried out through Gurudwaras, Sikh educational institutions and various religious congregations. He also organised killer squads in each village to eliminate the 'enemies' of the Sikh faith, thereby increasing his visibility and reach across the state.

Violence in Punjab escalated from 1982 to 1983 with attacks on policemen and political figures becoming the order of the day. Shaken by the scale of violence that had taken on a communal colour, Presidents rule was imposed in the state on 6 October 1983. Bhindranwale and his followers took refuge in the Golden Temple and the army was called upon to remove the militants in an operation mission codenamed 'Operation Blue Star' that lasted from 3-6 June 1984, and resulted in huge civilian and military casualties, as well as considerable damage to the temple.[2] The attack on the Golden Temple, considered the holiest Sikh shrine, was condemned by Sikhs all over the world and subsequently led to the assassination of the then Indian Prime Minister Indira Gandhi, by her Sikh bodyguards on 31 October 1984. This in turn resulted in violent riots and attacks against Sikhs that some blamed on the Congress party (Joint Enquiry Report into the Causes and Impact of the Riots in Delhi, 1984:1). The attack on the Golden Temple and the subsequent riots in which Congress was complicit broke the straw on the camel's back and catalysed the movement into a militant and violent campaign for a separate state.

Dealing with the Punjab Crisis

Following the unprecedented level of discontent whipped up by the army action in the Golden Temple, there was a major rethinking in government circles. The Indian government set about pursing a combined strategy of conciliation and force to stem the tide of terrorist violence and gain the confidence of the people in the state.

The Rajeev Longowal Accord. Realising the failures of Mrs. Gandhi's autocratic style of functioning, the Congress government under the new prime minister, Rajeev Gandhi (1984-89), began on a conciliatory note, although it remained committed to pursuing a hard-line policy towards the militants. The assault on the Golden Temple was recognised as a major error on the part of the central government even by the Congress leaders. Having gained a massive electoral victory, Rajiv Gandhi was more amenable to political concessions in Punjab including a settlement with the Akalis, which was crucial for any resolution that would prevent an escalation to the growing demands for a separate Sikh state. On their part, the Akalis realised that the continued radicalisation of Sikh politics would yield disastrous consequences for the Sikh community in India. Consequently, Sant Longowal, reinstated as head of the Akali Dal in 1985, pushed for a peace initiative, reiterating the importance of Hindu-Sikh amity, condemning acts of violence by Sikh extremists, and repeatedly declaring that the Akali Dal was not in favour of Khalistan. (Sharma, 1992: 105).

The Rajeev–Longowal accord signed on 24 July 1985 agreed to establish commissions and independent tribunals to resolve the Chandigarh issue and the river water disputes. Despite stiff resistance from extremist Akali factions, and leaders like the former Chief Minister, Prakash Singh Badal, and the leader of the SGPC, Gurcharan Singh Tohra, the accord constituted the first step towards restoring normalcy in the state. It also laid the basis for Akali victory in the coming elections. However, the fact that the demand for Chandigarh was still linked to Abohar and Fazilka, made the whole exercise futile. The centre appointed many commissions to examine the issue but could not work a satisfactory solution to suit both Haryana and Punjab. (Sharma, 1992: 117-23; Kohli, 1990: 370-71).

Within weeks of the accord, Longowal was killed by extremist elements who felt that he had sold out to the government. The successor government of Surjit Singh Barnala, which came to power in 1985, tried unsuccessfully to negotiate with the centre and the extremist factions, and was ultimately dismissed on 11 May 1987.

According to Hamish Telford,

> The Punjab crisis should have ended at this point, but the failure of Rajeev Gandhi's government to implement the accord undermined

> the legitimacy of the Barnala ministry and directly contributed to the revival of the militant movement which was soon suffering from acute factionalism. (1992:985).

Political Impasse and use of force. The dismissal of the Barnala government was used by the hardliners to revive militancy in the state. In the event, both the Congress and the Akali parties accused each other of aiding and abetting terrorism. To make matters worse, the Congress government at the centre adopted short-sighted policies to cover its own tracks. The fact that the Barnala government was dismissed on the eve of the election to the Haryana assembly, and President's rule promulgated on 11 May 1987, was not lost on the Sikhs. The timing of the dismissal stirred doubts about the centre's intentions and its desire to placate the Hindus in Haryana. According to Ved Marwah, Additional Commissioner of Police, Delhi, "it's not the acts of terrorism, but the panic response of the Government of India that achieved for the terrorists their aim of destabilising the political system." (1995:169).

Helpless against the growing violence and with no political solution in sight, the centre resorted to a series of military operations to curb militancy such as Operation Woodrose (1986-1987) and Operation Black Thunder (1988). However, force only aggravated the situation and guerrilla activities of the Sikh militants escalated after 1987.

The Centre could make no headway on the political front which alone could have brought about some improvement in the situation on the ground. Political initiatives under the V.P Singh government (December 1989 to November 1990) and the Chandrashekhar government (November 1990 to June 1991) also failed. The atmosphere grew even more vitiated after the general elections of 1989 that bought to power extremist leaders such as Simranjit Singh Mann, Attinder Pal Singh (leader of the Khalistan Liberation Organisation); and Bimal Khalsa (the widow of the assassin of Indira Gandhi) in Punjab. Emboldened by the election results, the militants issued orders demanding conformity with a new set of rules that forbade the consumption of alcohol, cigarettes, and meat at weddings; banned skirts and insisted that school uniforms be in particular colours of religious significance; and stressed the promotion of the Punjabi language (Baweja, 1992: 31).

External Support. The movement for the formation of an independent Sikh state also found support in the Sikh diaspora. Overseas Sikhs deeply affected by the attack on the Golden temple in 1984, were instrumental in the formation of numerous Sikh organizations outside India that came to be actively involved in collecting funds and organising training camps for the militants. Extremist organisations such as the National Council of Khalistan, Babbar Khalsa International and Dal Khalsa flourished in different parts of the world, particularly in the US, Canada, Italy, Denmark, Holland, and the United Kingdom.

These organisations found the support of extremist leaders, such as the late Ganga Singh Dhillon, a US national who headed the Nankana Sahib Foundation and declared the Sikhs to be a separate nation; and the late Dr Jagjit Singh Chauhan, a former medical practitioner, who put forth the demand for an independent Khalistan for the first time in 1971. To be carved out of the state of Punjab and Sikh dominated areas of Himachal Pradesh, Haryana and Rajasthan, Chauhan had grand visions of Khalistan as a state with its own currency, flag, passport, and stamps. (Nayar and Singh, 1984:145). In addition to the Sikh diaspora, Pakistan was also a crucial external player in the Khalistan crisis. The Indian government time and again pointed to the involvement of "a foreign hand", a veiled reference to Pakistan in abetting the movement. The White Paper on the Punjab Agitation prepared by the government of India had stated as early as 1984 that the militants were able to obtain sophisticated arms through sources outside the country and by developing clandestine links with sources within the country. It was suspected that militant organisations such as Khalistan Commando Force (KCF); Khalistan Liberation Force (KLF); and Khalistan Liberation Organisation (KLO) worked with each other and had strong links with Pakistan.

The government believed that there were large illegal flows of arms into India from across the border and that the terrorists were receiving different types of active support from certain foreign forces, but could not divulge more information for the sake of public interest (White Paper on the Punjab Agitation, 1984: 57). Though not much information is available on the logistics and arms provided to the insurgents, recovery of Chinese-made AKMs (popularly listed as AK-47 assault rifles) and RPGs pointed to Pakistan's involvement. India claimed that Pakistan provided Sikh secessionists with sanctuary, arms, money, training and moral support, and encouraged their demand for a separate homeland. The accusations against Pakistan began to increase in 1986-87 when the Government of India presented its case, based largely on circumstantial evidence, including broadcasts of the Pakistani media, interrogation reports, reports of trans-border encounters, and phone calls (Cronin, 1984: CRS-27). Armed intrusions across the Pakistani border, and interrogation of terrorists who were apprehended by Indian security forces, also revealed the existence of many militant training camps in such places as Sialkot, Gujranwala, Lahore, Kasur, Sargodha, Abbotaabad, Murree and Faisalabad.

Recruitment to terrorist ranks went up appreciably and the militants begun to exercise a greater role in the separatist agenda. To make matters worse, the Akali parties boycotted the elections and joined hands with militant organisations under a newly formed Shrimoni Panthic Action Committee comprising Kartar Singh Narang of the Babbar Akali Dal, Prakash Singh Badal, Baba Joginder Singh, father of Bhindranwale, and Manjit Singh of the All India Sikh Student Federation (AISSF). With the Akalis under their wing, the militants now launched an offensive against the Congress government. They initiated a campaign of boycott and coercion to disrupt the functioning of the government.

Back to normalcy: Cooperation between police and the army. Notwithstanding this, the centre persevered in its efforts to bring back normalcy in the state through political processes. The Congress party's election victory in 1992 marked a watershed in improving the situation in Punjab. In the elections, that had been boycotted by most parties in Punjab because it had been postponed for a year, Congress secured a three-fourths majority with just 9 per cent of the votes. With this victory, it set about the task of containing militancy in a very determined manner employing the help of the police, army, and para-military forces.

The strategies of K.P.S. Gill, the police commissioner, known for his aggressive tactics, and a "bullet for a bullet" approach, boosted the morale of the police force (Interview with KPS Gill, 28th May 1998). The stern measures employed by Gill were supported by the army, which provided invaluable help to the Punjab police under Operation Rakshak II to assist in anti-terrorist operations and create conditions for a free and fair election. While Gill's efforts sparked complaints of brutal excesses and tortures, militancy was effectively eliminated from Punjab by the end of 1992. The state had gained a decisive advantage over them through the intervention of the army and the police striking at the root of militancy. The major breakthrough came with the elimination of the Khalistan Liberation Force (KLF) chief, Gurjant Singh Budhsinghwala, Sukhdev Singh Dasuwal, the legendary chief of the Babbar Khalsa, and Talwinder Singh Parmar, of the Babbar Khalsa International, who was behind the fund-raising operations of the Babbar Khalsa International and had links with the Pakistani Inter Services Intelligence (ISI). The heavy hand used to curb militancy, and a growing rejection of violence amongst the people of the state marked the virtual end of the Khalistan movement.

While the measures taken from 1992 were critical in bringing to an end the demands for a separate state, it should be noted that the creation and sustenance of Khalistan as a viable independent state was a doubtful proposition to begin with. First, India was never going to accept an independent Khalistan, and resistance would have been futile simply because of the sheer size and might of India. Moreover, India's strategic interest in Khalistan was immense as any secessionist movement would have made India's frontiers vulnerable to outside powers and compromised the integrity and security of the country.

Second, even if Khalistan had been created, the economic and strategic challenges would have been insurmountable. Given its land-locked status, Khalistan would have been totally dependent on other powers, which would have severely compromised its capacity to trade and move goods and people independently. It could hardly have survived on agriculture, agro-industries, small-scale industries, foreign exchange remittances from emigrants, and skilled manpower as was envisaged by Jagjit Singh Chauhan (Masod and Stockdale, 1988: 141-42). More importantly, the creation of Khalistan on the basis of a Sikh identity was complicated by the fact that Sikhs and Hindus shared many traditions in terms of language and cultural practices (Kumar, 1995: 55-58). Therefore, the very conception of Khalistan was problematic, as it failed to recognise the interconnectedness of the Sikh and Hindu communities (Joshi, 1993: 18). Much of the strongest support for Khalistan came from its expatriate communities with individuals like Chauhan and Ganga Singh Dhillon taking the lead, and Khalistan essentially remained a vision nurtured with a passion by Sikhs who lived overseas. (Jeffrey, 1994: 211).

Why did the movement fail?. As argued earlier, it was the firm handling of the Centre, underlined by a mix of force and conciliation that had a major bearing on the direction and scope of the movement. There were several factors that contributed to the quelling of militancy in Punjab. The centre made repeated efforts to explore a number of options to work for a negotiated settlement of Punjab. The Rajiv-Longowal accord, coming as it did in the aftermath of the desecration of the Golden Temple was one such important step. However, the death of the moderate leader Longowal, and the difficulties associated with the implementation of the accord, made force a more effective alternative thereafter. Some points deserve mention in this regard. First, the effective co-ordination of the police and army operations was a major factor in quelling militancy in the state. The combined might of the state proved too strong for the Khalistan movement. The militants were hardly a match for the Indian state which had vastly superior forces numerically and in terms of resources. Second, the atrocities committed by the militants in terms of murder, rape, and extortion had alienated many of the ordinary people who, after a while, were not prepared to tolerate such actions in the name of Khalistan, especially when the terrorists began to target civilians regardless of their faith or denomination. The movement suffered a further setback when it was seen as being used by unscrupulous individuals and criminal elements who were interested mainly in personal profit (G. Singh, 1996: 63-74).

Third, Congress came into power at the Centre in 1992 and this played a vital role in transforming the situation in Punjab. The Congress government was committed to wiping out militancy from the state. The fact that Punjab was also controlled by Congress made things easier as the same party was in charge both at the Centre and the State. This facilitated better communication and cooperation between the state officials and the Central bureaucracy. (Joshi, 1993:19). Finally, support from Pakistan began to wane costing the movement its external support.

Some Conclusions

To sum up, the Punjab crisis was largely about the Sikhs' quest for more regional autonomy and identity. Political dithering and non-resolution of water and boundary disputes issues, compounded by the centralising policies of the Congress government, gradually led to widespread alienation among the Sikhs. Growing communal unrest and the upsurge of ethnic sentiments strengthened the claim for a distinct identity, with its extreme manifestation being the demand for Khalistan that tapped into the reservoir of ethnic mobilisation and plunged the state into violence for more than a decade.

The Khalistan movement endured during the 1980s for three important reasons. First, the centralising policies of the state had already sown the seeds of discontent among the Sikhs that led to a deep sense of alienation among the Sikhs. The support for the cause of Khalistan by the Sikh people, outraged by the attack on the Golden Temple in June 1984 and the massacres of the Sikhs that followed the assassination of Mrs Gandhi later that year, was almost inevitable in the given circumstances. Second, the movement had a strong base from a developed organisational infrastructure which comprised *inter alia* several militant outfits such as the Khalistan Commando Force (KCF), Khalistan Liberation Force (KLF), and Khalistan Liberation Organisation (KLO). Third, external support from the Sikh diaspora in the US and UK, as well as from Pakistan, which was allegedly providing Sikh secessionists with sanctuary, arms, money, and training, helped to sustain the movement for sometime.

However, once the state started deploying, by the late 1980s and early 1990s, the army, the federal police, and the paramilitary forces, through a series of well-planned operations to overcome the militants, the movement came under relentless pressure. The State also gradually gained the confidence of the people through sustained political negotiations and conciliatory policies. The combination of force and conciliation gradually put in place new political alignments in the state paving the way for normalcy.

Finally, the lack of unequivocal, external support for an independent Khalistan was a major setback to the movement's plans. In particular, Pakistani support, under increasing pressure from the West, declined considerably making it harder for the movement to stay alive. Even if external support was available, it could do little in the face of the virtual annihilation of the leadership and the complete control exercised by the federal government. The militant organizations on their part lost the support of the people once their membership had begun to attract lumpen elements that joined the movements for the lure of money rather than the long cherished cause of a separate homeland for the Sikhs and indulged in wanton rape and killings in the rural areas. Incarceration and the killing of prominent militant leaders further weakened the organisational structure of the movement and made it susceptible to suppression by the federal agencies. By 1991, the entire movement had begun to lose direction. It was the combination of all these factors singly and collectively that irretrievably weakened the militant forces and led to the ultimate demise of the separatist movement in Punjab.

Notes

1. In India's hierarchical caste system, the lowest position was occupied by people referred to as untouchables, and they were treated as outcasts and discriminated against socially, economically and politically. To redress this injustice, the Art 341 of the Indian Constitution provides that certain castes, races or tribes may be deemed as scheduled castes for special protection and privileges.
2. The actual figures are hard to determine with any certainty, with estimates varying from the official numbers of around 500 to the upper end of up to 5000 (Jeffrey: 1994: 181; Deol: 2000: 107).

References

Annexure D. (1984). "Sikh Agitation for Khalistan, Genesis of the Agitation" (Note prepared by the Home Ministry). In Kuldip Nayar and Khushwant Singh, *Tragedy of Punjab: Operation Blue Star and After* (New Delhi: Vision books Pvt. Ltd.

Baweja, Harinder (1992). Living by the Gun. Seminar, 39, October.

Cronin, Richard P. (1984). Crisis in Indian Punjab: Evolution, Issues, Competing Positions and Prospects", Report No. 84-152 F, Congressional Research Service, Library of Congress (August).

Deol, Harnik (2000). Religion and Nationalism in India: The Case of the Punjab, London: Routledge.

Gill, Sucha S. (1988). Development Crisis in Agriculture and Its Political Implications—An Enquiry into the Punjab Problem. In Wallace and Chopra (Eds), Political Dynamics and Crisis in Punjab, (pp. 436-450). Amritsar: Guru Nanak Dev University.

Gupta, Dipankar (1996). The Context of Ethnicity: Sikh Identity in a Comparative Perspective, New Delhi: Oxford University Press.

Jeffrey, Robin (1994). What's Happening to India, Punjab, Ethnic Conflict and the Test for Federalism, New York: Holmes and Meir Publishers.

Joshi, Manoj (1993). Combating Terrorism in Punjab, Indian Democracy in Crisis. Conflict Studies, 261, May. (Reproduced in

Ghosh, Partha ed. (1997) Rivalry and Revolution in South and East Asia: Aldershot, England: Ashgate Publishing Ltd.

Kaur, Kuldeep (1999). Akali Dal in Punjab Politics: Splits and Mergers. New Delhi: Deep and Deep Publications.

Khwaja, Sarfraz H. (1980). Sikhs of the Punjab 1900-1915: A Study of Confrontation and Political Mobilisation, Ann Arbor: Michigan University Microfilms.

Kohli, Atul (1990). Democracy and Discontent, India's Growing Crisis of Governability, Cambridge: Cambridge University Press.

Kothari, R. and Deshingkar, G. (1985). Punjab: The Long View. In Abida Samaiuddin (Ed.), The Punjab Crisis, Delhi: Mittal Publications.

Kumar, Pramod (1995). Violence in Punjab. Seminar, 434, October: 55-58.

Marwah, Ved (1995). Pathology of Terrorism in India, New Delhi: INDUS.

Masod, Maqsood A. and Stockdale, Peter (1988). The Khalistan Riddle. Islamabad: Modern Book Depot.

Nayar, Kuldip and Singh, Khushwant (1984). Tragedy of Punjab: Operation Blue Star and After. New Delhi: Vision Books Pvt. Ltd.

People's Union for Democratic Rights and People's Union for Civil Liberties "Who are the Guilty? (1984). Report of a Joint Enquiry into the Causes and Impact of the Riots in Delhi from 31 October to 10 November, 1984, Delhi.

Puri, Harish K., Judge, Paramjit S. & Sekhon, Jagrup S. (1999). Terrorism in Punjab: Understanding Grassroots Reality, New Delhi: Har-Anand Publications.

Sharma, Yog R. (1992). State Autonomy and National Integration: Identity Crisis of the Sikhs, Jammu: Vinod Publishers and Distributors.

Singh, Gopal (1984). Socio Economic Bases of the Punjab Crisis. *Economic and Political Weekly,* 19 (1) (January): 42-47.

Singh, Gurmit (1991). History of Sikh Struggles Vol. 2, Appendix 22, New Delhi: Atlantic Publishers.

Singh, Gurpreet (1996). Terrorism-Punjab's Recurring Nightmare. New Delhi: Sehgal Book Distributors.

Singh, Khushwant (1991). A History of the Sikhs, Volume 2, 1939-88. New Delhi: Oxford University Press.

Singh, Mohinder (1988). The Akali Struggle, A Retrospect. New Delhi: Atlantic Publishers and Distributors.

Telford, Hamish (1992). The Political Economy of Punjab, Creating Space for Sikh Militancy. *Economic and Political Weekly*, 32 (11), (November): 971-87.

Tully, Marc and Jacob, Satish (1985). Amritsar: Mrs Gandhi's Last Battle. London: Jonathan Cape.

White Paper on the Punjab Agitation (1984). Government of India: New Delhi.

6

WHY THE 1979 IRANIAN REVOLUTION DID NOT BRING AN ADVANCED MODE OF PRODUCTION WITH A REPRESENTATIVE AND REDUCED STATE POWER? A SOCIOLOGICAL EXPLANATION

MAHMOUD 'MAX' KASHEFI

Introduction

This paper offers an interpretation of why the outcomes of the 1979 Iranian Revolution were basically at variance with the demands of the initial uprising. During the last twenty-nine years, enough evidence has been published to substantiate the unexpected outcomes of the Revolution while minimal effort has been made to develop a sociological context within which the problem can be explained (e.g., Abrahamian, 1993; Ahmad, 1982; Arjomand, 1988; Bakhash, 1990). To that end, this paper illuminates the major demands of social classes at the initial uprising and compares them with the outcomes. To *explain* the variation, the paper also sheds further attention on the sociological debate whether a revolution "comes" or "happens." If a revolution happens, that is, different social classes pursue their own demands the outcomes of a revolution can be different from the primary demands of individual social groups. In contrast, if a revolution is made, the outcomes should be *predictable* based on the intentions of the vanguard groups which launched the revolution in the first place. More specifically, the paper argues that the Iranian Revolution *was not made* by Khomeini's "charismatic leadership." Rather, it was originally started by the popular uprising of social classes, especially the new middle class, who were under structural strains for decades, without having a clear image of the upcoming alternative socio-political system.

Following Goldstone's (1993) "developing process" of social revolutions, this paper differentiates three phases in the Iranian Revolution. Goldstone states that a revolution is a "developing process" in which the preconditions or causes, orientation and organization, and the outcomes of the uprising should be separately analyzed. First, the factors affecting each phase are not necessarily the same. Objective demands rather than subjective values normally stimulate popular uprising. However, the existence of objective demands does not necessarily result in a social revolution unless the people have their own *explanation* for the conditions, as well as organization to challenge the system causing their hardships. This is the second phase in which the leaders and vanguard organizations can play a significant role in the success or failure of a social revolution. Finally, the outcome of revolution has its own dynamic caused by new factors, such as conflicts and power struggles among formerly coalitional groups. Separating these phases highlights the spontaneous and architectonic aspects of social revolutions. The paper applies this model to the 1979 Iranian Revolution to *explain* and substantiate the proposition that Iranian upheaval originally resulted from structural strains. It was only during the second phase of the uprising that Khomeini's leadership emerged—who skillfully lead the movement toward the "Islamic Republic of Iran." After a theoretical discussion on the process of social revolutions, the paper covers the pre-revolutionary socio-economic conditions within which the Revolution started.

Then, it elaborates on the weaknesses of popular political organizations, especially the leadership vacuum, to explain why Khomeini emerged as the leader in the second phase of the Revolution. The last part covers the outcomes, with an emphasis on their variations with the initial demands. The paper ends with a short conclusion, including the theoretical and substantive significance of the findings.

Theories of Social Revolutions

Revolutions are not made, Skocpol (1979) says, they happen. Revolutions are not begun by revolutionary elites, with or without an organized and ideologically imputed mass followers. Rather, in certain structural crises, masses start revolting for concrete demands different from the ideology of the "marginal elite." In this sense, social revolutions are not "rationally orchestrated and engineered" social changes. Rather, they are more or less emotional *reactions* to structural strains imposed by a regime and cannot be substituted by social reforms. In contrast to Skocpol's structural theory, modernization theory (Tilly, 1978; Green, 1982) gives a prime role to counter-elites who mobilize people against the existing social and political system—counter-mobilization. Consistent with the modernization theory, Milani says "making revolutions are artistic action." Revolutions do not come as some structuralists believe, rather, they "are made by the deliberate policies and heroic actions of committed revolutionaries" (1985: 34). Or, they are made by the "unlimited creativity of the human mind" (Najmabodi, 1993: 199). Therefore, the modernization perspective, unlike Skocpol's structural theory, connotes a consciously designed process of revolution in which the elites and their ideology play a significant role in the success of social revolutions. So does the Marxian perspective, in which revolutions are made by the social classes who have gained their class consciousness and have been mobilized by the vanguard parties against the dominant classes and the preexisting mode of production. Meanwhile some experts refuse to generalize and prefer to make a typology of revolutions. Huntington's

(1968) Eastern and Western type of revolutions, Arjomand's typology (1993) of "Tocquevillian and Aristotelian-Paretian models," and Dix's (1983) "Varieties of Revolution," are samples of work which try to make distinction between various revolutions.

The Iranian Revolution in 1979 stimulated the preceding debates by challenging some of the primary propositions on which most theories of revolution are based. Examining the socio-economic realities of Iran, Skocpol pointed that "[i]n Iran, uniquely, the revolution was 'made'... through a set of cultural and organizational forms thoroughly socially embedded in the urban communal enclaves" (1982: 275). However, she fails to explain why the outcomes of a "self-consciously" made-revolution become at variance with its initial popular demands. Ahmad (1982) criticizes Skocpol and says that "emphasis on Iran's Islamic avocation and the Ulama's [clergies] key role in Iranian politics is exaggerated and misleading" (1982: 295). He adds that, in fact, all revolutions have had a combination of both spontaneous and architectural actions. The Iranian Revolution, however, comes closer to the "revolutions-that-come" than anyother third world revolutions (1982: 299). Ahmad, however, does not specify how and in what phase of its evolving the Iranian Revolution was made or happened. Milani challenges both Skocpol's and Ahmad's theory on the nature of Iranian upheaval. He says "making revolution is a creative art" (1985: 179) and it was the "Khomeini's charismatic leadership" that made possible "the Islamic revolution of Iran." Milani's focus is apparently on the second phase of the Revolution. His discussion basically ignores the initial popular demands and the unexpected outcomes of the Revolution. Therefore, the Iranian Revolution provides a new opportunity to expand prevailing theories of social revolutions. The following section, applying Goldstone's "developing process" combined with Skocpol's view, elaborates on the initial demands of the Iranian uprising to contrast them with its astonishing outcomes to substantiate the spontaneity of the Revolution.

Phase 1: The Preconditions of the Iranian Revolution

The initial demands of modern middle class. Most Iranian scholars fairly believe that the 1979 upraising was initially started by the modern middle class who were suffering from socio-political strains for decades. "Among the contending forces, the middle class was [the] most prepared to lead the Iranian revolution: It had not only quantitative superiority but also qualitative advantage over both the upper and lower classes" (Amirahmadi, 1988: 225). The Iranian modern middle class was developed as a direct result of modernization. Their subculture had been deeply shaped by the Westernization of the country's infrastructure since the 1905 Constitutional Revolution. Therefore, their general focus was on democracy, freedom, and civil rights, rather than religion, which was considered as a private matter of life. In May 1977, fifty-three lawyers, taking advantage of the Shah's sudden liberalization, signed an open letter in which he was accused of being an authoritarian ruler and asked for political reforms and reviving people's rights.[1] In June 1978, three popular figures of the National Front wrote a letter accusing the regime of devastating the economy and violating international law, human rights, and the Iranian constitution. In the same month poets, novelists, and intellectuals denounced the regime for violating the constitution and demanded an end to the censorship. Since June 1978, numerous movements, open letters, public lectures, strikes, and demonstrations were launched by the modern middle class demanding political and social reforms, including free elections, respect for the constitution, improving economic conditions, and an end to corruption. Based on observations and evidence, the initial uprising demands were basically reformist yet deeply structural, the actions were generally spontaneous yet carefully measured, and the movements were originally secular and socio-political rather than religious or ideological (Tehranian, 1979). The modern middle class, understanding the historical significance of the situation and the crises, started to move for their social and political demands. Neither Khomeini nor any other leader *made* them to raise their voice or arms for an Islamic or any other forms of government.

The initial demands of the merchant capitalists (bazaaries). As the Shah's regime followed industrialization, and spurred a strategy of development without political reforms, the bazaars' power started to diminish. The bazaars' prosperity mainly depended upon the flow of foreign imports and investments. The increasing role of modern economic organizations (banks, supermarkets, etc.) hurt bazaaries and caused their economic strains (Green, 1982; Amjad, 1989). The Shah made the following remark: "the bazaaries are a fanatic lot, highly resistant to changes." "I could not stop building supermarkets. I wanted a modern country. Moving against the bazaar was typical of the political and social risks I had to take in the drive to modernization (Pahlavi, 1980: 156). Experiencing economic hardships caused by the Shah's modernization's efforts, the bazaaries started a life-and-death struggle against the regime and actively participated in the Revolution. Their alliance with religious leaders and their financial support of the Revolution effectively damaged the Shah's regime. The merchant capitalists, thus, were motivated to fight against the Shah's regime and his modernization policies because of their *social and economic* interests rather than merely for the dismissal of Islamic values.[2]

The initial demands of the working class. With the ascendancy of modernization and the economic boom of the early 1970s, the industrial working class emerged as the largest urban class in the seventies. The total labor force was 10.6 million in 1977. Out of this number 2.5 million, or 23.5%, worked in the industrial sector (Amjad, 1989: 111). Despite the increasing proportion of the working class, they did not pose any serious threat to the Shah's regime for a few reasons. The working class was a heterogeneous group without any working class culture or "collective consciousness." Furthermore, the workers were only allowed to enter the labor unions created by the state. Such unions were created as a support base for the regime rather than to deal with the grievances of workers against their employers. Finally, the government followed some labor policies that benefited the workers, such as insurance for workers, numerous housing projects, and the minimum wage standards (Milani, 1985: 111). The regime's policy paid off as the workers were among the last groups who joined the uprising. Their demands were originally economic in nature, but later gradually changed to political, such as removal of martial law and the freedom of all political prisoners. By October 1978, 45% of their demands were political, reaching to 80% in November and 100% in February 1979 (Bayat, 1988). Of the many strikes, those by the electrical workers created periodic power blackouts in Tehran and "forced many factories to shut down and layoff their workers" while the oil workers "deprived the government of much needed oil in the cold winter" (Milani, 1985: 204). The working class protests were precipitated by the economic recession starting in the late 1975. By the mid summer 1978, the real wage of workers started to fall, unemployment rose from "almost nothing to nearly 400,000 and take home pay in construction industries slumped as much as 30%" (Abrahamian, 1982: 511).

None of those three major social classes thus wanted to establish a theocracy. Their demands were structural reforms or removal of the Shah as the main obstacle to the reforms. Their respect for religion "was drawn out and nourished as an idiom within which the Shah could be opposed" (Green 1982: 89). Furthermore, the ethnic minorities, like Azerbaijanis, Arabs, and Kurds became Khomeini's supporters not because they were crying for an Islamic Republic or "religious symbols and ideals" as Skocpol says. Rather, they were willing to support any effective anti-Shah political groups with the power to stimulate widespread social changes, including greater cultural autonomy for the ethnic minorities. "Their commitment to Khomeini was to a force capable of stimulating political change rather than to a religious leader" (Green, 1982: 89). Finally, when Khomeini established his undisputed leadership and offered his Islamic Republic, *yet not officially taken the leadership of the state*, portrayed the Islamic State as a progressive and civilian system within which basic human rights are guaranteed for all people. The massive demonstration of Ashura (December 11, 1978), organized and supported by Khomeini's followers, declared a seventeen-point resolution substantiate the preceding proposition. The resolution included: "The social, political and legal rights of all members of the society, religious minorities and other nationals living in Iran;" "true freedom, honor and human dignity of women, as granted by Islam, as well as social rights and the opportunity for the full development of all their capacities should be provided and secured;" "guarding of our national independence and integrity, and provision of individual and social freedom;" "enforcement of social justice and security of the rights of workers and peasants, and provision of the opportunity for their full enjoyment of the fruits of their labor;" and many more (OIMS, 1979: 42).

The popular demands intertwined with economic-political crises. The existence of the preceding popular demands and the socio-political strains did not lead to the Revolution until a few other conditions emerged. The popular demands intertwined with several economic and political crises, on the one hand, the development of public *perception* that the Shah is the cause of the strains and the Islamic Republic is the trusty alternative, on the other hand. Crises in the Shah's political system began as the result of pressures exerted by the Carter administration. However, it is naive to assume that the massive upheaval of various social classes was the direct result of President Carter's human rights policy without understanding the interactions of structural strains and the pressures from abroad. James Davies' theory of the J-curve and social revolution contends that "revolution is most likely to take place when a prolonged period of rising expectations and rising gratifications is followed by a short period of sharp reversal, during which the gap between expectations and gratifications quickly widens and becomes intolerable" (1979: 415). The economic conditions in Iran during 1970-1978 firmly substantiate this thesis. Non-oil GDP increased from $16.3 billion to $30.5 billion (adjusted dollars) from 1970-1976. Per capita income rose from $550 to $1600 during the same period. The previous deficit gave away to an impressive $2 billion surplus in 1975 and the net foreign assets of the government exceeded $7.7 billion (Milani, 1985: 166). The oil boom of the early1970s provided a golden opportunity for Iran's economic expansion. Between 1964 and 1974, Iran's cumulative oil revenue came to $13 billion and topped $38 billion during 1974 to 1977 (Abrahamian, 1982). The oil boom, however, was short and there was a sharp drop in oil prices in the international oil market during 1977-1978. As a result, the surplus of $2 billion in 1974 was turned into a $7 billion deficit in 1978. State expenditures dropped $6.9 billion in 1977 and $10.2 billion in 1978, leading to a huge increase in unemployment. The wholesale and retail trades' annual growth rate declined from 13.5% in 1975 to only 7% in 1976-77 (Milani, 1985: 172). Despite the problems the Shah pursued his policies of "toward great civilization." To spur these policies he increased the salaried middle class' taxes, establishing price stabilization, and extending the policy of "private-public ownership" which, in turn, deepened the economic crises and expanded it into social and political crises.[3] Finally and more importantly, the privatizing policy which required the sale of privately-owned shares up to 49% and publicly-owned shares up to 99% created a sense of *insecurity* among the upper class who had been the government's allies (Kamerava, 1989). The policy divided the upper class and marked the beginning of the *capital flight* out of the country.

In the midst of economic crises came political pressures from the Carter administration and Amnesty International for greater liberalization and political freedom which intensified the unrest. In response to the international criticism of his regime, the Shah initiated a liberalization policy in early 1977. The state-controlled media freely published materials deemed treasonous only a year earlier. The Shah declared that political prisoners would not be tortured and ordered security forces to be tolerant toward dissidents. Western observers were allowed to attend the trials of dissidents (Abrahamian, 1982; Milani, 1985) The reforms, however, were too late and the strains, accumulated for decades, have already provided "fertile soil for discontent and radical challenges to the regime" (McDaniel 1991: 218) within which the modern middle class "sparked off the revolution, fueled it, and struck the final blows" (Abrahamian, 1982: 533). Merchant capitalists, the working class, and the ethnic and religious minorities later joined the movement and finally brought the upheaval to a successful social revolution.

Phase 2: Leadership Organization and Orientation

This period is the most critical phase of a revolution. Not only the success or failure of a revolution depends on the dynamic of this conjuncture but also the outcomes of a successful revolution as determined by the goals and ideals of the person/organization which emerges as the leader. In the Iranian Revolution this phase (1978-1979) emerged when the people realized that the Shah's decision-making ability had been paralyzed. Changing prime ministers one after another, arresting and sacrificing many former friends (including Prime Minister Hovida and General Nasiri the head of Secret Services) not only did not save the Shah, but instead helped the opposition groups to understand the significance of the conjuncture for a profound structural social change. Furthermore, President Carter's human rights policy not only disintegrated the regime but *psychologically* promoted the opposition. The people *perceived* that the USA's unconditional support of the Shah had changed and that the Shah was being pressured by the Carter administration to reform the system. Such *perception* gave the modern middle class a new lease on life, strengthening the spirit of defiance among them. Finally, the Shah received contradictory signals from the USA's State Department and from the National Security Council (NSC). The former was for a peaceful resolution of the crises and the latter for an iron-fist approach. Facing this new revolutionary situation—but mostly unprepared—neither the National Front nor the Left were able to establish their leadership status and thus Khomeini became the undisputed leader of the Revolution.

How Khomeini's leadership did emerge. The National Front was the only major political organization with a nationwide network, managerial skills, and political legitimacy to govern the state. Representing the aspirations of the modern middle class, they had the greatest potential to emerge as the vanguard of the Revolution but failed for a few reasons. First, their leaders were unable to upgrade and harmonize their slogans with the public demands. Their agenda for revolutionary Iran was the constitution, with limited authority for Shah's and more political freedom for the people. This advocacy of reforms diminished their ability to cross classes and expand beyond their constituency. The same reform rhetoric was offered by the Freedom Movement headed by Bazargan, peaceful campaigns through constitutional means. Bazargan, speaking to a huge crowd at Tehran University, admitted their weakness in that revolutionary situation: "Don't expect me to act in the manner of [Khomeini] who, head down, moves ahead like a bulldozer, crushing rocks, roots and stones in his path. I am a delicate passenger car and must ride on a smooth, asphalted road" (Bakhash, 1990: 54).

Unlike the reformist demands of the National Front, the Left was asking for a revolution. However, despite their uncompromising position and dedication, especially Fadaiyan-e-Khalq and Mojahedin-e-Khalq, the Left failed to organize and to orient the masses and thus to emerge as the leader for several reasons. Their brutal suppression by the regime cost them heavily. More than 90 percent of their founders and the original members were executed or killed by the Shah's regime by 1976 (Amjad, 1989). They were obsessed with guerilla activities instead of working among the masses to prepare them for a popular uprising. As a result, when the Revolution started they were not in a position to mobilize or organize the people. They lacked nationally recognized and experienced leaders while Iranian culture always demanded an individual figure rather than a vanguard party or organization. Finally, and probably the most importantly, the Left suffered from cultural alienation. They used political languages developed in the Bolshevik revolution or in Latin American Marxism, not attractive for the people who had been socialized with Islamic values for many centuries. Consequently, the Left's supporters were mostly limited to high school and college students, some intellectuals, and a small percentage of the modern middle class and working class.

Khomeini's leadership had *emerged* as a popular alternative at this conjuncture for several reasons. It bears keeping in mind that Khomeini and his followers fearlessly tried to *make* a revolution in 1963, but they failed (Arjomand, 1988). In the 1977 uprising, however, Khomeini "seized power by riding on the waves of a successful mass revolution" (Dorraj, 1990: 24) since young urban Iranians, who started and fueled the Revolution, knew so little about him. During the socio-political crises of 1977-1979, while the masses were testing and looking for a trusted leader, two precipitating factors significantly helped Khomeini's leadership. First, Khomeini's oldest son died in Iraq of a heart attack. When the news spread throughout Iran, it was popularly *perceived* to be the work of Shah's Secret Services. The people who were fed up with the regime wanted to blame it for any unpleasant events. This perception portrayed Khomeini as a crusader who was determined to end the Shah's regime regardless of the costs involved.[4] Second, a letter appeared in the Tehran daily (*Etela'at*) attacking Khomeini in a vicious manner. The regime, by unsubstantiated charges against Khomeini, in fact, "inadvertently recognized, formalized, and legitimized him as the opposition leader" (Green 1982: 85). In this context, the Shah significantly contributed to Khomeini's eventual leadership. Rather than ignoring him, the regime unwittingly elevated him to the status of a hero while contributing to his legitimacy. According to Green, by publishing the letter, the "regime itself helped to convert reformist protest into outright revolution" (1982: 85).

In addition to those precipitating factors, several other factors helped Khomeini to gain leadership status of the Revolution. Unlike his street followers, he acted rationally and crossed class lines which made him a skillful populist rather than a fundamentalist. He avoided making public announcements that would alienate some of the oppositions—issues like vice-regency of Islamic jurist (Velayat-e-faqih). Instead, he attacked the regime on topics that outraged all segments of the opposition, such as corruption, the decay of agriculture, the increasing cost of living, the suppression of newspapers and political parties (Abrahamian, 1982: 532). Furthermore, he was able to gain the support of radical intellectuals and students by stressing such themes as exploitation and anti-imperialism. He promised to "liberate the country from foreign domination," to extend "freedom to all political parties, even atheistic ones," to guarantee the rights of all religious minorities, and to bring social justice to all" (Abrahamian, 1993). These promises, especially through informal channels and with ordinary language, were familiar for the masses. They were "designed in terms of archetypical legends of Persian historical memory" (Tehranian, 1979: 10). Therefore, the populist themes of the promises expressed in the people's language and culture succeeded in winning over a wide range of social classes and characterized the Revolution as essentially multi-class populism. *Consequently, Khomeini emerged as the legitimate leader of the Revolution and started to orient the masses toward his utopian Islamic Republic.*

Phase 3: Outcomes of the Revolution

The modern middle class aspirations suppressed. Ironically, democracy, freedom, and civil rights that were the focus of the modern middle class, as the pioneer of the Revolution, have not been invoked but suppressed. During the1990s, Iran was ranked number one among nations in terms of holding and torturing political prisoners. More recently, *The Economist* reported "the number of executions nearly doubled last years [2006] to 177, bringing Iran the unsavory distinction of being the world heaviest user of capital punishment per head population" (Aug. 25, 2007). At least 13 juvenile offenders were executed in the last five years, more than any other nations (Human Rights Word Reports: January 2007). Amnesty International reported that more than five thousand people were executed in Iran during 1987-1990 and more than 50% of them were activist modern middle class and students (*Iran Times*: December 1990). Suppression of the new middle class made Iran number one in "brain drain" in the world (*Iran Times*: January 2003). Human Rights Watch Report's of Iran in 2006 declared that Iranian authorities, under the leadership of

Supreme Leader Ali Khamaenei, "systematically suppress freedom of expression and opinion by closing newspapers and imprisoning journalists and editors." Because of suppression many "writers and intellectuals have left the country, are in prison, or have ceased to be critical." The Islamic Government "systematically blocks websites inside Iran and abroad that carry political news and analysis." Since Ahmadinejad came to power in 2005, the authorities have used "prolonged solitary confinement, often in small basement cells, to coerce confessions and gain information regarding associates." During 2006 "the authorities intensified their harassment of independent human rights defenders and lawyers in an attempt to prevent them from publicizing and pursing human right violations." Ethnic and religious minorities have been subject to discrimination and persecution. For example, the regime denies "Iran's Baha'i community permission to publicly worship or pursue religious activities." In May 2006, "Iranian Azeris in the northwestern provinces of East and West Azerbaijan and Ardebil demonstrated against government restrictions on Azari language and cultural and political activities. Security services forcibly disrupted public protests and engulfed the region...four people died in clashes in the city of Naghadeh on May 25." (Human Rights World Report, January 2007). The same suppression documented in Freedom House reports: "The Iranian government continues to violate the civil liberties of its citizens. In July 2005 Iran's judiciary officially acknowledged widespread violations of prisons' rights,...solitary confinement, imprisonment without charge, and torture continues to be reported." "On university campuses, students' demonstrations are often attacked by student members of the paramilitary Basij organization or by outside vigilantes" (Countries at the Crossroad 2007, Iran). To silence Shirin Ebadi (the 2003 Nobel Peace Laureate), the Iranian interior ministry recently announced that the CDHR (Center for Defense of Human Rights; co-funded by Ebadi) is illegal and any "activity by this center is illegal, and violators of this decision will be prosecuted." According to Human Rights Watch reports, "if Ebadi is threatened for defending human rights, then no one who works for human rights can feel safe from government prosecution" (Human Rights Watch, August 8, 2006).

The triumph of merchant capitalists (bazaaries). The Shah's White Revolution in 1962 witnessed the demise of the merchant economy and formation of industrial capitalism in which the old class structure of Iran was dismantled. The overthrow of the Shah's regime in 1979 again brought merchant capitalists back into power. The statistics given by the Islamic Republic indicated that most industrial firms collapsed or were operating under 50% of their capacities after the Revolution. More than seven thousand industrial projects were blocked by the new bureaucracy as the result of the bazaaries' influence in the government (*Iran Times*, November 1990). By taking advantage of the government subsidies and cheap currency (up to 20 times lower than the market value) the bazaaries gained billions of dollars each year and, consequently, many industrial factories were shut down (*Iran Times*: October 1992). According to Zamani's fact-based reports, the average industrial investment rate dropped from 15% (during 1959-1977) to 1% (during 1977-2000). On the other hand, the ratio of liquidity to real GDP, reflecting the growing rate of short-term investments, increased from 15.8% in 1979 to 244.4% in 1991 and to 573.3 in 2001 (Zamani, 2004). More importantly, the percent of GDP invested by foreign nations dropped to less than half a percent during 1993-2004, compared to the average 14% for the other underdeveloped nations and 28% for the developed countries (Zamani, 2004).

Mafia type of economy emerged. The economic outcomes of the Revolution were not limited to the collapse of the industrial investments; rather the system provided opportunities for an underground/Mafia-type of economy that benefited the coalition of Ulama-bazaaries and their children (Agazadeh ha). Amuzegar (2003), the former member of the IMF Executive Board, reported that non-transparent and secretive financial transactions after the Revolution have allowed "the formation of private mafia" economy. Friedman's (2002) report substantiates the same conclusion: The Iranian system includes "vast monopolies awarded to their allies- the bazaar merchants, clerics and children of the clergy- as well as Islamic charities that serve as front organizations for huge business conglomerates that pay no taxes and import everything from cigarettes to cars, duty-free." (New York Times, June 24). The report adds that Iran cannot attract industrial investors without some transparent rule of law, which means "curbing the arbitrary rule of the Guardian Council of clerics and the judges they appoint, who sit atop the system" (June 22, 2002). Such a Mafia-type of economy is labeled "clientelism" in Alamdari's (2005) research; a mode of economy organizes "people into rival groups and clique- or clan-types of relations" (p. 1289). The system is based on patron-client interests which is also the source of the political power structure of the society.

> Financially, patron-client organizations are self-sufficient because they either have Charity and endowment incomes or officially receive allocated budgets from the government, or both. Easy access to allocate oil revenue and unchecked trade activities have provided some religiously privileged groups with unique opportunities to form autonomous politico-economic bounds. More than 60% of Iran's foreign trade takes place outside government administrative rules. Some of these groups have been involved directly in foreign trades owning their own ships and ports that bypass the customs department and that are guarded by their own armed men (2005: 1291).

The working class is the main loser. The Islamic system drastically worsened the working class' conditions. The International Alliance in Support of Workers in Iran (IASWI) reported that the "country faces a major crisis of unprecedented dimensions. Not only the wages of 1998 have not been paid in full, many workers have received no wages for 1999." "The government itself admits that in more than 500 factories' salaries have not been paid for over a year and in some cases for more than two years." "Inflation is such that even if three time current wages were paid in full and on time, workers would still find it difficult to feed of a family of three." Minimum monthly wages were set a 36,500 Toomans (approximately $50), while even based on the government's own estimates a family of three requires an income of 120,000

Toomans ($170) a month in order to cover basic needs. "Labour protests rose from 188 in previous year to 244 episodes [major protests only]," "more than 70% of the protests were concerned mainly with the demand for payment of wages (124 episodes)." "Frustration in their fight for trade union rights and economic demands, forcing the workers to recognize that the normal forms of economic struggle are unlikely to bear fruit" (Abkhun and Yekta, 2007). Osanloo, the executive committee of the *Syndicate of Workers of Tehran and Suburbs Bus Company* (SWTBC) and now in the custody of regime, declares:

> Increasing inflation, shrinking wages and exclusion of various workshops from the supervision of existing labor laws, based on legislative memoranda, guidelines, and the bills passed by the fifth, sixth, and seventh Parliament, assaults on protesting workers who demanded their unpaid wages, crushing of labor demonstrations by the security police,... submission of the employed workers to deteriorating work conditions to prevent summary termination, the growing numbers of unemployed causing fear among workers to demand their rightful earnings... creation of disappointment and hopelessness among the workers of low literacy, experience, and skills resulting in growing rates of substance abuse to escape mental and spiritual despair, especially among the job-seeking youth and lower echelons of society...(Vahed Bus Drivers website, February 2007).

Summary and Conclusion

The 1979 upheaval emerged as a collective response to the Shah's absolutist role during the late 1970s political, social, and economic crises. It was not launched by Khomeini or any other vanguard organizations. Rather, it was spontaneous, started by the modern middle class for their socio-political demands—independence, democracy, and socio-economic justice—*not for* religious values or symbols. Khomeini's leadership emerged in competition with nationalism and Marxism-Leninism during the *second phase* of the Revolution. The outcomes, however, demonstrated that the demands of the *most* parties who participated in the Revolution were not realized. The Islamic Republic neither established an advanced mode of production nor provided a participatory political system for which the people revolted. Baazaries and Ulama were the ultimate winner of the Revolution. Neither the new middle class, who started the uprising at the first place, nor the working class, who paralyzed the Shah's regime, nor the ethnic minorities, who were asking for their autonomy, materialized their demands. The Iranian Revolution revealed that a revolution, in many aspects, is destructive rather than being constructive. The second phase of the Revolution, in fact and unlike the first phase, was emotionally orchestrated collective behaviors. The Revolution "like a forest fire, a hurricane, or a tornado," (Nomani and Behdad, 2006) came and Khomeini, a fundamentalist while acting as a populist, crossed the class lines and gained the power, but the publics acted under illusions and only after the Revolution did they realize that they "were asking for rain instead they got flood."

The significance of this study is not limited to its theoretical contribution, helping to explain the dynamic of the Iranian Revolution and its possible generalization; rather, it offers substantive results for activists who have devoted their life for socio-political transformation of their societies. The outcomes of revolutionary social changes are not *necessarily a progressive socio-political system with a transparent state*, as revealed in this case study. Rather, rationally orchestrated social reforms have potentiality to bring a more accountable/transparent regime with predicable and reliable outcomes than emotionally lunched social transformations. This study revealed that if a regime is stubborn and resists against any reformist social changes and, consequently, the public upheaval becomes inevitable (it *happens*) the role of activists become "fault finding," especially during the second phase of the uprising. The success or failure of an uprising, and more importantly its outcomes, depends on the ideology and mentality of an approaching leader. The populist rhetoric should not mislead the publics and activists as evident in the Iranian case. While there is a strong potentiality in a revolutionary uprising to be destructive because of its emotionally lunched nature, one should not generalize that all revolutions are destructive as did Akbar Ganji, the most prominent political Iranian dissident. The major lesson we learned from the Iranian revolution is not to have another revolution, "the Iranian revolution was not hijacked by anybody...The nature of revolution creates a reign of fear—a cycle of fear. It's been repeated in every revolution" (Conversation with History, UC Berkeley; August 2006).

Notes

1. This open letter is addressed to a person who, a few years ago at Harvard University, declared, "[t]he outcome of the violation of individual freedoms and disrespect for the spiritual needs of human beings is frustration. And frustrated individuals will follow the path of rejection to cut themselves off from all social rules and traditions. The only way to eliminate these frustrations is to respect individual freedoms and to believe in the truth that the people are not the slaves of government, but government the servant of the people..." "Therefore, the only way to restore and nurture the personality of individual, to establish national cooperation, and to escape from the problems that threaten Iran's future, is to abandon authoritarian rule, to submit completely to constitutional principles, to revive people's rights, to respect the Constitution and the Universal Declaration of Human Rights, to abandon the single party system, to permit freedom of the press and freedom of associations, and to establish a popularly elected government based on the majority will" (Siavoshi 1990: 135).
2. The bazaars' financial well-beings had direct effects on Ulama (clergies). Bazaaries were traditional and paid their religious taxes and other contributions directly to Ulama. Therefore, Ulama started battling against the Shah's regime because they were losing both their economic resources and their social status. Ulama, in fact, started suffering from the gradual demise of two economic resources—the demise of Bazaaries payments and the cuts of the regime's religious subsidies from $80 million to $30 million, thus increasing their motives to turn against the Shah's regime (Benard and Khalilzad 1984: 203).
3. Taxes for the salaried middle class increased from $2.02 billion in 1975 to $5.86 billion in 1978 and more than 17,000 merchants and shopkeepers were arrested and taken to the courts because of price violations (Milani 1985).

4. People gradually stared acting emotionally; e.g., a widespread rumor started that "Khomeini's picture had been seen in the moon!"

References

Abkhun, Yusef and S. Yekta (2007). The Labour Movement in Iran: A Year of Increasing Protest. *International Alliance in Support of Workers in Iran, www.workers-iran.org/article5.htm*

Abrahamian, Ervand (1982). *Iran between Two Revolutions,* Princeton: Princeton University Press.

——(1993). *Khomeinism: Essays on the Islamic Republic.* Berkeley, University of California Press.

Ahmad, Eqbal (1982). Comments on Skocpol. *Theory and Society,* Vol.11: 293-300.

Alamdari, Kazem (2005). The power structure of Islamic Republic of Iran. *Third World Quarterly,* Vol. 26: 1285-1301.

Amirahmadi, Hooshang (1988). "Middle-class Revolutions in the Third World." In H. Amirahmadi (ed.) *Post Revolutionary Iran;* Boulder, Westview Press.

Amjad, M. (1989). *Iran: From Royal Dictatorship to Theocracy.* New York: Greenwood Press.

Amuzegar, Jahangir (2004). Iran's Unemployment crisis. *Middle East Economic Survey (MEES),* Vol. XLVII. No. 41.

Arjomand, S. A. (1986). Iran's Islamic Revolution in Comparative Perspective. *World Politics,* Vol., 38: 383-414.

——(1988). *The Turban for the Crown: The Islamic Revolution in Iran.* NY: Oxford Press.

——(1993). Plea for an Alternative View of Revolution. *Contention,* Vol. 2 # 2: 171-183.

Bakhash, Shaul (1990). *The Reign of the Ayatollahs: Iran and the Islamic Revolution.* New York: Basic Book Inc. Publisher.

Benard, C. and Zalmay Khalilzad (1984). *The Government of God: Iran's Islamic Republic.* NY: Columbia University Press.

Bayat, Assef (1988). "Labor and Democracy in Post-Revolutionary Iran" In H. Amirahmadi (ed.) *Post Revolutionary Iran;* Boulder, Westview Press.

Davies, C. James (1979). The J-Curve of Rising and Declining Satisfactions As a cause of Revolution and Rebellion. Davis Grahm and Ted, R. Gurr (eds), *Violence in America: Historical and Comparative Perspectives,* Beverly Hills: Sage Publications.

Dix, Robert (1983). Variations of Revolutions. *Comparative Politics,* 15: 281-294.

Dorraj, Manocheher (1990). *From Zarathustra to Khomeini: Populism and Dissent in Modern Iran,* Boulder: Lye Rienner.

Freedom House (2007). "Country Report: Iran", *http://www.freedomhouse.org/*

Friedman, Thomas (2002). "The Clerics' Days are Numbered." *New York Times.* June.

Goldstone, A., Jack (1993). Predicting Revolutions: Why We Could (and Should) Have Foreseen the Revolutions of 1989-1991 in the U.S.S.R. and Eastern Europe. *Contention.* Vol. 2 # 2:127-151.

Green, Jerald (1982). *Revolution in Iran: The Politics of Counter-Mobilization.* New York: Praeger Publishers.

Huntington, S. (1968). *Political Order in Changing Societies.* New York: Yale University Press.

Iran Times (1990-1994). "Articles on the Islamic Republic of Iran." *International Iran Times.*

Kamrava, Mehran (1990). *Revolution in Iran: The Roots of Turmoil.* London: Routledge.

McDaniel, Tim (1991). *Autocracy, Modernization, and Revolution in Russia and Iran.* New Jersey: Princeton University Press.

Milani, Mohsen (1985). *The Making of Iran's Islamic Revolution.* London: West View Press.

Najmabadi, Afsaneh (1993). "States, Politics, and the Radical Contingency of Revolutions" In *Research in Political Sociology.* Vol. 6:197-215.

Nomani, F. and S. Behdad (2006). *Classes and Labor in Iran: Did the Revolution Matter?* New York: Syracuse University Press.

OIMS (1979). *The Rise: Leaflets in English.* A Publication of Organization of Iranian Moslem Students. Vol. 5: Appendix 1.

Pahlavi, Mohammad Reza (1980). *Answer to History.* New York: Steen and Day.

Siavoshi, Sussan (1990). *Liberal Nationalism in Iran: The Failure of a Movement*. Boulder: Westview Press.

Skocpol, Theda (1979). *States and Social Revolutions: A Comparative Analysis of France, Russia, and China*. Cambridge: Cambridge University Press.

——(1982). "Rentier State and the Shi'a Islam in the Iranian Revolution", *Theory and Society*. 11: 65-84.

Tehranian, Majid (1979). "Iran: Communication, Alienation, Revolution", *Intermedia*, Vol. 7: 6-12.

Tilly, Charles (1978). *From Mobilization to Revolution*. Reading, Mass.: Addison-Wesley.

Zamani, Hadi (2004). "Opportunities and Challenges for Iranian Globalization", *www.iransolidarity.com*

INDEX

Y & Z